THE STORY
OF SLAVERY
AND ABOLITION
IN UNITED STATES HISTORY

IN
UNITED STATES
HISTORY

★ LINDA JACOBS ALTMAN ★

Enslow Publishers, Inc.
40 Industrial Road
Box 398
Berkeley Heights, NJ 07922
USA

http://www.enslow.com

Library of Congress Cataloging-in-Publication Data
Altman, Linda Jacobs, 1943–
    [Slavery and Abolition In American History]
    The story of slavery and abolition in United States history / Linda Jacobs
Altman.
        pages cm. — (In United States history)
    "Originally published as Slavery and Abolition In American History in
    1999"—Title page verso.
    Includes bibliographical references and index.
    ISBN 978-0-7660-6330-3
    1. Antislavery movements—United States--History—Juvenile literature.
    2. Slavery—United States—History—Juvenile literature. 3. Fugitive slaves—
    United States—History—Juvenile literature. 4. Abolitionists—United
    States—History—Juvenile literature. I. Title.
    E449.A1557 2015
    973.7'114—dc23
                                        2014025960

Printed in the United States of America

Future Editions:
Paperback ISBN: 978-0-7660-6331-0
EPUB ISBN: 978-0-7660-6332-7
Single-User PDF ISBN: 978-0-7660-6333-4
Multi-User PDF ISBN: 978-0-7660-6334-1

To Our Readers: We have done our best to make sure all Internet addresses in this book were active and appropriate when we went to press. However, the author and the publisher have no control over and assume no liability for the material available on those Internet sites or on other Web sites they may link to. Comments can be sent by e-mail to comments@enslow.com or to the address on the back cover.

♻ Enslow Publishers, Inc., is committed to printing our books on recycled paper. The paper in every book contains 10% to 30% post-consumer waste (PCW). The cover board on the outside of each book contains 100% PCW. Our goal is to do our part to help young people and the environment too!

Illustration Credits: ©Thinkstock/Denis Aglichev Collection/iStock , p. 1; ©Thinkstock/ Photos.com, p. 4; Enslow Publishers, Inc., pp. 59, 70.

Cover Illustration: ©Thinkstock/Denis Aglichev Collection/iStock

☆ **CONTENTS** ☆

Fugitive slaves running away from a plantation near the eastern shore of Maryland.

Chapter 1

A THOUSAND MILES FOR FREEDOM

In December 1848, a frail Southern gentleman boarded the train at Macon, Georgia. Stooped and slow-moving, he was obviously in poor health. It was as if every step caused him great agony. His right hand was wrapped in a heavy bandage, and the lower part of his face was hidden by a poultice tied under his chin.

His only companion was a black slave, who showed remarkable concern for his ailing master. As was the custom of the time, the slave rode in the "Negro car" at the back of the train. The master traveled in a luxurious compartment with several other white gentlemen. He was not much of a conversationalist. While the others discussed cotton, slaves, and other topics of interest to Georgia slaveholders, the invalid stared out the window at the passing countryside. Even when someone spoke directly to him, he did not react. The men figured he must be deaf, or nearly so, and left him alone.

The gentleman and his slave got off in Savannah and made their way to a first-class hotel. Except to see that the invalid was made comfortable in his room, the hotel staff paid little attention to the new arrivals. They would have been shocked had they known the truth of their identity.

The "invalid gentleman" and his slave were actually William and Ellen Craft, a married slave couple making a desperate bid for freedom. They had planned the disguise with great care. Ellen was light-skinned and could pass for white, but that alone would not have been enough. In the South of 1848, well-bred ladies did not travel alone with male slaves. So Ellen became Mr. William Johnson. The bandaged face hid her lack of a beard; the bandaged hand, her inability to read or write. A gentleman who could not sign his own name would have aroused suspicion in the class-conscious South.

From the beginning of their dangerous adventure, the Crafts traveled in style, figuring that no one would expect an escaping slave to stay in first-class hotels and eat in fine restaurants. The ruse worked well until they arrived in Baltimore and tried to buy tickets to Philadelphia, in the free state of Pennsylvania.

Southerners were suspicious of anyone who wanted to take a slave into a state where slavery was not legal. Abolitionists (people who wanted to end slavery) had been known to take outrageous risks to smuggle runaway slaves to freedom.

William Craft had settled Ellen in "one of the best carriages" and was heading for his own car when an officer asked where he was going:

"To Philadelphia, sir," I humbly replied.
"Well, what are you going there for?"
"I am travelling with my master, who is in the next carriage, sir."

"Well, I calculate you had better get him out; and be mighty quick about it, because the train will soon be starting. It is against my rules to let any man take a slave past here, unless he can satisfy them in the office that he has a right to take him along."[1]

The Crafts were terrified when the officer took them to the office. Their carefully planned disguise seemed about to fail them. All they could do was hope for the best and continue playing their parts. Fortunately, the other passengers in the depot were obviously outraged at this treatment of the "invalid gentleman." Just as the train was getting ready to pull away, the authorities relented and told "Mr. Johnson" he could pass.

Soon, the Crafts were safe in Philadelphia. That night, in a boardinghouse run by an abolitionist, the Crafts knelt down "and poured out our heartfelt gratitude to God, for his goodness in enabling us to overcome so many perilous difficulties, in escaping out of the jaws of the wicked."[2]

For every happy outcome like that of the Crafts, there were probably dozens of tragedies—people who lived and died as slaves in a system that dehumanized and exploited them because of the color of their skin.

THE PECULIAR INSTITUTION

Slavery has existed in some form throughout human history, most often as a by-product of war. Victorious armies would often plunder enemy treasures and enslave whole populations. The ruling classes then used this captive labor force for everything from building pyramids to tending vineyards.

In the fifteenth century, slavery began a transformation that would change the fate of empires. It became a business. Slave traders journeyed to Africa, where they captured or bought people to sell as slaves in Europe and in the New World.

Some three hundred years later, the plantation culture of the American South made slavery a way of life. The "peculiar institution," as Southerners called slavery, shaped their society.[1] The result was a culture split into two realities: one for black slaves, another for white masters.

Slaves lived with untold brutality and suffering while many of their masters created a fairy-tale world of dashing gentlemen, demure ladies, and lavish hospitality. Before that world came to an end, it would plunge the United States into the bloodiest war of its history.

The Atlantic Slave Trade

Early in the fifteenth century, Portuguese explorers heard stories of a river of gold, somewhere in "the lands of the blacks of Guinea."[2] Unimaginable riches waited for anyone brave enough to seek this undiscovered country, and clever enough to find it.

The intrepid Portuguese began exploring the West African coast in 1434. They never found a river of gold. What they did find was slaves—black Africans who could be kidnapped in raids or bought from black traders who did not mind dealing in human flesh.

For centuries, Africans had followed the practice of enslaving captives of war. They also sold criminals, with slavery substituting for prison time. In some tribes, people would hand over their unwanted children as payments for debt.

By 1448, Portuguese slavers had transported about a thousand Africans to buyers in Portugal and the Portuguese islands of the Azores and Madeira.[3] The slave trade proved to be profitable, with plenty of eager buyers willing to pay high prices for workers they could own as property.

The trade spread over much of Europe and then to the New World. On January 22, 1510, King Ferdinand of Spain opened the New World to African slavery by sending fifty men to work in the gold mines of Hispaniola (a Caribbean island, now divided between the nations of Haiti and the Dominican Republic). That was just the beginning. The floodgates opened, and by the eighteenth century, "fully six of every seven people who arrived in the Americas were African slaves."[4]

The profitability of slave trading attracted dealers from Great Britain and the Netherlands (Holland). British involvement began in 1562, with a voyage by Captain John Hawkins. New to the trade, Hawkins was bold in his methods of acquiring new slaves. He kidnapped some, purchased a few, and stole the rest from Portuguese slavers. Hawkins then sailed to the New World, where he managed to sell some three hundred slaves to eager buyers on Hispaniola.

The Dutch slave trade began more slowly. In the 1590s, a group of Amsterdam businessmen brought slaves from Africa, only to be forbidden to sell them on the grounds that slavery was immoral. Slavery never did catch on in the Netherlands itself, but Dutch dealers did a thriving business with the New World. It was a Dutch ship that made the first known sale of African slaves in what would become the United States. In 1619, tobacco grower John Rolfe of the Jamestown Colony recorded the purchase of "twenty Negroes" from a "Dutch man of war."[5]

By 1725, people from America were sending their own ships to Africa, hoping to get in on the rich profits. The first slave port in the colonies was at Providence, Rhode Island. Later, the slave trade also operated through ports in New York, Maryland, and South Carolina.

Slavery existed in all the thirteen colonies, but it did not thrive in the North, where industry was gradually becoming more important to the economy. The South was another matter. Rather than build factories, Southerners planted cotton and tobacco, crops that require a great deal of physical labor. They got that labor by using slaves.

Slave trading was a thriving industry in America by 1776, when Thomas Jefferson's ringing words proclaimed "that all men are created equal; that they are endowed by their Creator with certain inalienable rights; that among these are life, liberty, and the pursuit of happiness."[6]

From Africa to the New World: A Slave's Odyssey

The process of obtaining, transporting, and selling slaves began and ended with the worst sort of brutality. After being torn from their homes, the captives were chained, then force-marched to the coast. Sometimes they had to walk for weeks, with barely enough food and water to survive. They were lashed if they moved too slowly, left to die if they fell by the wayside. Those who made it were locked up in coastal fortresses called "factories," to languish there until European traders came to buy them.[7]

By the eighteenth century, more than a hundred of these slave factories operated along the Gold Coast (present-day Ghana). One of the best known factories, Cape Coast castle, could hold up to fifteen hundred men, women, and children in its filthy, underground slave holds.

The Atlantic crossing, or "middle passage," as it came to be called, was even more torturous than the factories. Under good sailing conditions, the voyage took an average of forty to fifty days; under bad conditions, it could be much longer. Journeys of two to three months were not uncommon. One of the longest recorded voyages took nine months to travel from Africa to the Caribbean, losing fifty-five slaves along the way.[8]

English abolitionist Robert Walsh described a typical slave ship, which had set out from Africa with 562 slaves aboard:

> She [the ship] had been out seventeen days, during which she had . . . fifty-five [deaths]. The slaves were all enclosed under grated hatchways, between decks. The space was so low, that they sat between each other's legs, and . . . there was no possibility of their lying down, or at all changing their position, by night or day. . . . The space . . . was divided into two compartments, 3 feet 3 inches high; the size of one was 16 feet by 18, and of the other 40 by 21; into the first were crammed the women and girls; into the second, the men and boys. . . . We also found manacles; and fetters of different kinds, but it appears that they had all been taken off before we boarded.[9]

Though slaves did represent an investment of money and, therefore, had value as property, there was rarely any concern for them as living human beings. In 1738, for example, the Dutch slave ship *Leuden* smashed into some rocks with more than seven hundred slaves aboard. There was no way the crew could control so many. Terrified of dying at the hands of their own cargo, the crew of the *Leuden* locked the hatches to the slave decks and abandoned ship, leaving 702 people to drown.

Even more cold-blooded a man was Captain Luke Collingswood of the British slaver *Zong*. He ordered 133 sick slaves thrown alive into the sea because the ship's insurance would pay for lost cargo, but not for dead human beings.

Slaves who survived the voyage next faced the ordeal of sale. There were many ways of bringing slave sellers together with potential slave buyers. In Rio de Janeiro,

Brazil, dealers displayed their merchandise in huge showrooms along a street called Vallongo, which became known as the Avenue of Tears. In Charleston, South Carolina, slaves were marched from the docks to an open-air market in back of the post office.

In some ports, a "scramble" was the preferred method of sale. Instead of going to a public market, dealers set fixed prices and sold slaves directly from the ship. On the day of the scramble, potential buyers gathered on the docks like marathon runners waiting for the starting gun. At a signal, they dashed aboard and began a frantic search for the best "bargains."

Slavery in Colonial America

Colonial slavery developed within a world that was accustomed to unfree labor: "until the nineteenth century unfree status of one type or another—slavery, serfdom, peonage—was the lot of much of humankind," wrote historian Peter Kolchin.[10] In the colonies, the demand for unfree labor was "largely color-blind."[11]

Until the 1680s, African slaves were rarely seen in all American colonies, south as well as north. Colonists filled their labor needs with indentured Europeans. Some indentured servants were petty criminals, sentenced to serve a certain number of years working for a colonial master. Others came voluntarily, usually in exchange for passage to the New World.

Indenture had some advantages for both parties. The servant had a chance to build a new life, and the master got a much-needed worker, along with a valuable bonus: a land allotment (usually fifty acres) per person transported. It was Great Britain's way of building a colonial population while also creating a landed gentry (upper-class property owners) to rule that population.

In practice, indentured Europeans were often treated as badly as African slaves. Class-conscious Great Britain had little patience for "the 'lower ranks,'" whether they were rebellious Celts from the Irish countryside, "'rowdy' elements" from the London slums, or dark-skinned "savages" from the African jungles.[12] The supposed inferiority was more a matter of social class than of race.

The transition from indenture based on social class to slavery based on race began in the 1680s. Colonists could not get enough indentured servants to fill their ever-growing labor needs. This was especially true in the South. Landowners wanted to grow staple crops such as tobacco, rice, sugar, and cotton. These crops required vast acreage, which the Southerners had—and a huge labor force, which they did not have.

There has been much argument about the connection between racism and African slavery. Did racial prejudice lead to the enslavement of Africans, or did the enslavement of Africans lead to racism? Most modern authorities agree that there was no direct line of cause and effect. Instead of one causing the other, racism and slavery interacted to produce a system with a twisted logic all its own: Africans were racially different from Europeans, *and* Africans were enslaved by Europeans; therefore, Africans were inferior to whites and well suited for slavery.

"Racism does not create slavery. It is an excuse for it," said historian J. H. Plumb. "Racism was a . . . feature of the centuries when slavery was being established in America and it was, therefore, easy to make it one of the justifications for the institution."[13]

By the mid-1700s, African slavery had taken firm root in the South, and though it also existed in the North, it was not widespread. Unlike the agricultural South, the North was slowly becoming an urban (city) area and developing an industrial economy. Instead of slaves, who were difficult to control in cities, Northern employers began to rely on cheap immigrant labor to staff their factories and shops.

By 1790, the United States Census recorded 657,527 African slaves in the South, but only 40,370 in the North. By 1860, the difference between the numbers would be even more dramatic: 3,953,696 slaves in the South, and only 64 in the North.[14] Those figures reflect the differences that would eventually tear the nation apart and leave a heritage of racism to plague future generations.

PEOPLE AS PROPERTY

After the American Revolution, the system of slavery became more entrenched in the South and more controversial in the North. Southerners defended it, a growing number of Northern liberals opposed it, and slaves themselves made heroic efforts to defy it.

Down on the Old Plantation

Slavery and plantation agriculture grew up together, beginning in Virginia, Maryland, and parts of North Carolina, where tobacco was the crop of choice. Tobacco was well suited to the climate and the soil, but it had one drawback: Growing it profitably required a large force of cheap, unskilled labor. For white Southerners, cheap labor meant slave labor. Slavery freed the planters from daily toil, giving them the leisure to shape Southern life.

The plantation culture was more like the European feudal estates of the Middle Ages than the bustling, workaday world of the cities in the Northern states. The cultural layers of the white South tended to be rigid. At the bottom of the social scale were poor whites who owned neither land nor slaves. Next up the ladder was the independent farmer who owned a small plot of land, and perhaps owned half a dozen slaves. Often, these masters worked in the fields with their slaves. The "middling" farmers came next, their status determined by owning more land and more slaves (fifteen to fifty) than the group beneath them.[1] Finally, there was the planter aristocracy: some three thousand wealthy families, each owning more than one hundred slaves.[2]

On the surface, the planters' world was beautiful. It has been stereotyped as elegant, gracious, and above the industrial drudgery that was the norm in Northern cities. Even today, the term "Old South" calls forth images of dashing gentlemen, delicate ladies, and magnolia blossoms scenting a sweet Southern breeze. In the background of that picture, mostly out of sight, were the black people who lived in poverty and pain so their masters could live in luxury.

The Movement Begins

The years immediately after the American Revolution saw the beginning of an abolition movement in the North, which worked to abolish, or get rid of, slavery. The Pennsylvania Society for the Abolition of Slavery was founded in 1784, under the leadership of Benjamin Franklin, Alexander Hamilton, and John Jay. A year later, Jay became president of the newly formed New York Manumission (to free from bondage) Society. Ten years later, these two societies joined to create a national organization, known as the American Convention for Promoting the Abolition of Slavery and Improving the Condition of the African Race.[3]

These groups believed that the institution of slavery would die under its own weight. Gradual emancipation (freedom) could take advantage of that trend, allowing time to educate the new slaves for the responsibilities of freedom.[4]

There were already signs that such an approach might work. For example, the Northwest Ordinance of 1787 had stopped the spread of slavery into the vast Northwest Territory, which included the present states of Ohio, Indiana, Illinois, Michigan, and Wisconsin.

In 1817, the American Colonization Society had a new idea for ending slavery: Free the slaves and send them back to Africa, where a free colony would be established for them. The idea was controversial from the beginning. Many American-born blacks opposed it because they had no ties to the African past. On the other hand, a surprising number of slave owners were in favor of the idea. They certainly did not want to free their slaves, but they did want to find a way to get rid of free blacks.

Free blacks simply did not fit into the Southern way of life. A black person without a master was a "bad example" to slaves, giving them ideas, making them discontented with their lot. The slaveholders could not tolerate that. They preferred a South where all whites were free, and all blacks were slaves. It would be easier to maintain order in such a society.

Only in regard to the Atlantic slave trade were the early abolitionists able to make an impact. With incidents like the *Zong* killings to fuel the fire, the brutalities of the trade became an international scandal.

Great Britain led the crusade against the African trade, but the United States was not far behind. After a long political, economic, and moral struggle, Great Britain banned the international slave trade on May 1, 1807. The United States followed on January 1, 1808.

Moderate abolitionists hailed the ban as the beginning of the end of slavery in the United States. The slave trade had all but disappeared in the North, and had never become established in the Northwest Territory. In the Upper South, hundreds of masters were voluntarily freeing some or all of their slaves. That was a start, the moderates told themselves; the rest would come in time.

Slavery as "a Positive Good"

Southerners were determined to keep their peculiar institution. For years they had struggled with moral conflicts about slavery. In the early 1800s, they began putting the conflicts aside. Instead of apologizing for slavery, they began to portray it as a positive social force that benefited all concerned: society, the master, and even the slaves.

The slave master became a father figure. This image of a stern but benevolent parent who cared about the welfare of his people soothed many a conscience. Not only did it allow the master class to enslave black people, but it let them feel good about doing it.

Charles C. Jones, a slave-owning Presbyterian minister living in Georgia, wrote a book to remind his fellow slaveholders that blacks "were placed under our control . . . not exclusively for our benefit but theirs also." Caring for their well-being was the master's duty: "[W]e cannot disregard this obligation thus *divinely imposed*, without forfeiting our humanity, . . . and our claim to the spirit of Christianity itself."[5]

Many slave owners disregarded this obligation, but some took it to heart. For example, this letter from a slave-owning father to one of his sons stressed a master's responsibility toward his slaves:

> [You] may enjoy the good things of this world & relieve many of your distress'd brethren.—feed the poor & clothe the naked—but always have in mind that our first charitable attentions are due to our slaves—cause the sick to be well nursed and attended—the young, aged, and decrepid [*sic*] to be clothed & fed with the same care as the most useful—the well to be treated with mildness humanity and justice—consider their situation and strive to make the bitter portion of slavery as comfortable as the local situation . . . will [allow]."[6]

The Stirrings of Freedom

All efforts at control were doomed to failure. Owners simply underestimated their slaves' will to be free. Black people resisted their servitude in many ways. The field hand who managed to be slow and ineffective enough to inconvenience the master without bringing punishment on himself was making a small protest against slavery. So was the house servant who became "all thumbs" whenever she handled the good china, and the laborer whose "clumsiness" damaged nearly every piece of equipment he touched.

A few brave souls went beyond this carefully disguised resistance to mount armed rebellions. In 1800, the blacksmith-slave Gabriel Prosser planned a revolt that terrified the state of Virginia.

Prosser was born a slave on Brookfield, a large plantation north of Richmond. During his childhood, he learned to read and write. Most slave owners considered literacy dangerous for a child born into bondage. A slave who could read was a slave who could ask uncomfortable questions and think uncomfortable thoughts. The next "mistake" was teaching him a skilled trade. Slaves with marketable skills tended to get restless.

By the age of twenty, Prosser was a strapping six feet three inches, with the barrel chest and well-developed arms of a man who worked all day at the forge, shaping and pounding red-hot metal. Such was Prosser's skill that his master hired him out to others who needed the services of a blacksmith. Prosser often worked in Richmond, where he experienced a world beyond Brookfield plantation.

It was a world of conflicting loyalties and strange politics, in which a black slave named Toussaint L'Ouverture had led a successful insurrection in the French colony of Saint Domingue (present-day Haiti). With his slave army, L'Ouverture overthrew the colonial government and seized control.

The victorious slaves created something new in the Americas: a colony of free black people, ruled by a black general of uncommon ability and courage. L'Ouverture's exploits inspired Gabriel Prosser—and terrified Virginia's white people, who feared nothing so much as a slave uprising.

Prosser began to think, and then to plan. He prepared to strike on the night of August 30, 1800. A sudden thunderstorm foiled his plan, dumping so much rain on the area that creeks flooded, bridges crumbled, and dirt roads became lakes of mud. Only a handful of rebels made it to the meeting place, leaving Prosser no choice but to wait until the following night.

Before the rebels could reorganize, they were betrayed by two slaves who had lost their nerve. Prosser and all of his chief lieutenants were arrested and were sentenced to hang. There is some confusion among historians about the exact date of Prosser's execution, but his death certificate was dated October 20, 1800.[7]

"Virginia authorities hoped that would be the end of it," wrote historian Douglas R. Egerton. "Many slaves believed otherwise. . . . The . . . magistrates had only hanged the man. They could not kill the dream."[8]

Another dream that would not die was the dream of a black nation in the New World. On January 1, 1804, Jean-Jacques Dessalines, successor to Toussaint L'Ouverture, proclaimed the free black Republic of Haiti, "the first country in the history of the world to be founded on the triumph of a slave rebellion."[9] The name was appropriate for the new nation—"Haiti" means a "higher place."

Chapter 4

MATTERS OF CONSCIENCE

The 1820s was a decade of controversy, compromise, and violence where slavery was concerned. It was also a time of religious revival, when many Americans sought spiritual and moral renewal. The issue of slavery nibbled at the edges of many people's consciences. How could a person of faith stand idly by while fellow human beings were traded as property? This question laid the foundation for the militant antislavery movement that began in the 1830s.

"The Wolf by the Ears"

Long before there was an organized abolition movement, the conflict between slave states and free states (where slavery was illegal) simmered beneath the surface of American politics. The South wanted to expand and extend slavery; the North wanted to restrict it.

Northern opposition to slavery was based more on practical grounds than on moral ones. The spread of slavery would give more political power to the South. This could be a problem when the interests of the agricultural

South conflicted with the goals of the increasingly industrialized North.

These conflicts came into the open in 1818, when Missouri petitioned to enter the Union as a slave state. This raised serious issues for opponents of slavery. Not only would a new slave state upset the existing balance of twenty-two states with eleven on each side of the issue, but it would set a dangerous precedent. If one new state could allow slavery, what would stop the next state from allowing it, too?

Pro-slavery and antislavery forces argued for two long years. The confrontation was finally settled with the Missouri Compromise of 1820. This law allowed slavery in the new state of Missouri and in western territories acquired through the Louisiana Purchase below the 36°30' parallel. Slavery would be illegal in future Louisiana Territory settlements above that line of latitude.

At best, the Missouri Compromise was only a stopgap measure. It did not solve the fundamental problem. Most Northerners had no intention of tolerating slavery forever, and Southerners had no intention of giving it up.

Former President Thomas Jefferson, who had served from 1801 to 1809, elderly by then and long retired, understood the conflict from the inside out. In principle, he had always opposed slavery; in practice, he continued to own slaves. He knew that the South would pay for its stubborn loyalty to an institution that was fast becoming extinct in the rest of the world: "We have the wolf by the ears," he once wrote to a friend, "and we can neither hold him, nor safely let him go. Justice is in one scale, and self-preservation in the other."[1] It was a good summary of the dilemma that ate at the heart of Southern culture.

Every so often, the "wolf" would howl, as when Gabriel Prosser shook the power structure of Virginia with a rebellion that never really got started. In 1822, a former slave named Denmark Vesey did the same thing in South Carolina. Like Prosser, he was betrayed by slaves who told their owners of his plans. He died on the gallows on July 2, 1822, another casualty of the struggle against slavery.

The Second Great Awakening

The roots of the nineteenth-century abolition movement lay partly in the religious revival known as the Second Great Awakening. (The first "Great Awakening" had swept the country during the colonial period.) The leading figure of this movement was Charles Grandison Finney, a preacher with a flair for evangelism and a passion for social justice.

Finney denied the old Puritan belief that "God decided an individual's spiritual fate even before birth. . . . [W]hile God demanded that all His children adhere strictly to the letter of His law, nothing that any of them said or did could alter the predestined fate of their souls."[2] This grim Christianity had little room for joy and even less room for social reform. It encouraged fear, dread, and passive acceptance of "God's will," whatever that might be. Finney, instead, called for individual responsibility, not only in spiritual matters but in earthly ones as well.

His uncompromising stand on slavery turned many an eager Christian into a committed abolitionist. Finney wrote:

> Are we to hold our peace and be partakers in the sin of slavery, by [our connivance]? God forbid. We will speak

of it, and bear our testimony against it, and pray over it, and complain of it to God and man. Heaven shall know, and the world shall know, and hell shall know, that ye protest against the sin, and will continue to rebuke it, till it is broken up.[3]

The emphasis on social reform gave evangelical Christians, such as Baptists and Methodists, common ground with the Society of Friends (Quakers). Beginning in 1755, Quakers became the first group in history to ban slaveholding as a matter of principle. Quakers such as Lucretia Mott, John Greenleaf Whittier, and Sarah and Angelina Grimké played a big role in making abolition a national issue.

In 1828, Quaker abolitionist Benjamin Lundy convinced a young Baptist named William Lloyd Garrison to devote his energies to "the cause of the slave."[4] That proved to be a historic achievement. Garrison would become the leader who rallied the antislavery troops and laid out the strategies for them to follow.

The Passionate Abolitionist

At the beginning of his public career, William Lloyd Garrison favored gradual emancipation, to give the slaves time to adjust to their new freedom. That opinion soon fell by the wayside. At heart, Garrison was not a man to be gradual about anything.

In January 1831, he launched *The Liberator*, a weekly newspaper that would last for thirty years, becoming the chief national forum for the abolitionist cause. In the first issue, Garrison took his stand and made his vow:

In Park Street Church, on the Fourth of July, 1829, in an address on slavery, I [thoughtlessly agreed] to the popular but pernicious [deadly; destructive] doctrine of *gradual* abolition. I seize this opportunity to make a full . . . recantation.

I *will* be as harsh as truth, and as uncompromising as justice. On this subject I do not wish to think, or to speak or write, with moderation. No! No! Tell a man whose house is on fire to give a moderate alarm . . . —but [do not] urge me . . . to use moderation in a cause like the present. I am in earnest—I will not equivocate—I will not excuse—I will not retreat a single inch—and I WILL BE HEARD.[5]

William Lloyd Garrison's stand did not make him a popular figure, even in the North. He advocated not only the end of slavery, but full equality for black people and for women.

According to biographer Henry Mayer, Garrison "inspired two generations of activists—female and male, black and white—and together they . . . achieved a social change that conventional wisdom first condemned as wrong and then ridiculed as impossible."[6]

The Slave Who Had Visions

In 1800, Nat Turner was born a slave on a plantation in Southampton County, Virginia, and was later sold to Joseph Travis. From earliest childhood, Nat Turner was highly intelligent and imaginative. The slaves marveled at his abilities; many believed he was destined to become a religious prophet.

In adulthood, Turner became a slave exhorter (lay preacher), honored for his spiritual wisdom. At the age of twenty-five, he claimed he had what he could only describe as a vision: "I saw white spirits and black spirits engaged in battle, and the sun was darkened—the thunder rolled in the Heavens, and blood flowed in streams—and I heard a voice saying, '*Such . . . you are called to see, and let it come rough or smooth, you must surely bear it.*'[7]

In a later vision, he said he saw

> drops of blood on the corn, as though it were dew from heaven . . . and I then found on the leaves in the woods hieroglyphic characters and numbers, with the forms of men . . . portrayed in blood, and representing the figures I had seen before in the heavens.[8]

These brutal visions provoked equally brutal acts. In the predawn hours of August 22, 1831, Nat Turner and seven other slaves broke into the home of Turner's owner and killed all five members of the sleeping family.

The rebels moved on, gathering supporters as they went, stopping to slaughter whites wherever they found them. By the time the killing spree ended on August 23, Nat Turner and his men had murdered "nearly 60 whites."[9]

Stunned by the bloodshed, slave owners had a glimpse of something they did not want to acknowledge: Keeping an entire people in subjugation was dangerous. Some Virginians began to wonder whether the system was worth the risk of preserving it.

In the end, white Virginians could not bring themselves to give up their peculiar institution. Instead, they concentrated on eliminating opposition to it. Within days of the Southampton uprising, they captured or killed all of Nat Turner's followers. Turner was not captured until October 30. After dictating his famous confession from his prison cell, he was tried on November 5 and hanged on November 11, 1831.

Nat Turner's rebellion triggered new and stricter laws all over the South, along with new restrictions on the rights and liberties of free blacks. Frightened white leaders went to great lengths to stifle any criticism of slavery. Some states even made it a crime to circulate William Lloyd Garrison's *Liberator*.

The American Anti-Slavery Society

In the winter of 1833, William Lloyd Garrison called abolitionists to a meeting in Philadelphia. *The Liberator* had reached many new people with the abolitionist message, he said. It was time to form a national organization to carry the struggle forward.

More than sixty people from eleven states came to that first meeting. By the time they left, they had become charter members of the American Anti-Slavery Society. They planned to organize local abolitionist groups throughout the free states of the North, produce and circulate antislavery literature, and pressure religious leaders to take up the cause of the slave.

A top priority of the organization in those early years was to recruit and train lecturers who could take the antislavery message to church and civic groups all over the North. That task fell to ministerial student Theodore Dwight Weld. He did not have to look far for candidates. A strange sequence of events had provided more than he would need.

In 1834, Weld triggered an uproar at the Lane Theological Seminary by holding a series of student-led antislavery debates. Seminary president Lyman Beecher was not pleased. His way of dealing with the issue of slavery was to avoid it altogether. He expected his students to do the same.

For breaking that unwritten rule, Weld was dismissed from the seminary. A good portion of the student body went with him. From these idealistic dropouts, Weld chose the Anti-Slavery Society's famous "Band of Seventy."

Before the society's seventy went into the world, Weld drilled them in abolitionist theory. He covered the "history, philosophy, and profitability of slavery, the biblical arguments for and against [it], and also introduced . . . black speakers, who [explained] the effect of prejudice on their lives."[10]

Theodore Weld was not the only abolitionist whose life was shaped by the uproar at Lane. Seminary president Lyman Beecher's married daughter Harriet was profoundly affected by it. For the first time, she began to think about the problem of slavery. Some eighteen years later, Harriet Beecher Stowe would write *Uncle Tom's Cabin*, the antislavery novel that challenged the conscience of a nation.

The Racist Backlash

As the abolitionists made inroads in their battle against the peculiar institution, defenders of slavery appealed to nineteenth-century racism to justify their society. The arguments were already old: People of color were racially inferior to whites; their cultures were "primitive," "savage," or worse; their religions were flat-out wrong. These attitudes were not limited to the South; they flourished in the North as well, as many African Americans were to learn.

John Malvin, a free black from Virginia, went to Ohio in 1827, hoping to find a place where he might be accepted. He was bitterly disappointed:

> I thought upon coming to a free state like Ohio that I would find every door open to receive me, but from the treatment I received by the people generally, I found it little better than in Virginia. . . . I found every door closed against the colored man in a free State, except the jails and [prisons], the doors of which were thrown wide open to receive them.[11]

Ten years later, abolitionist leader Frederick Douglass would make similar observations about Philadelphia:

> There is not perhaps . . . a city in which prejudice against color is more [widespread] than in Philadelphia. . . . It has its white schools and colored schools, . . . its white Christianity and its colored Christianity, its white concerts and its colored concerts. . . . Colored persons, no matter how well dressed or well behaved, . . . are not even permitted to ride on any of the many railways through that Christian city.[12]

This shocked and disappointed those who expected nonslaveholding states to be free of bigotry. This was never the case, though. Many people in free states were just as bigoted as Southern slaveholders.

Harvard University professor Louis Agassiz was not a supporter of slavery, yet he became the "father of scientific racism" with his theories about the inborn inferiority of Africans: "Negroes were by nature submissive, obsequious [excessively obedient] and imitative. It was [wrong] to consider them equal to whites." To "prove" that this supposed inferiority was inborn, he noted that "Africans had been in contact with whites for thousands of years, yet were still [not affected by] civilized influences."[13]

Dr. Josiah Nott, a Southern "scientific racist," wrote that

> The Negro races stand at the lowest point in the scale of human beings, and we know no moral or physical agencies which can redeem them from their degradation [lower status]. It is clear that . . . any attempt to improve their condition is warring against an [unchangeable] law of nature.[14]

Both Agassiz and Nott went so far as to suggest that black people might not be simply a different race of humans, but a different (lower) species altogether.

Slaveholder Alexander H. Stephens, who would later become vice president of the Confederacy, claimed that this fundamental inferiority explained why "slavery—subordination to the superior race—is [the black person's] natural and normal condition."[15]

This outspoken racism infuriated the Garrisonians, who, in turn, infuriated the slaveholders with their attacks on both slavery and racism. By the end of the 1830s, abolitionist hopes for a peaceable end to slavery had begun to fade. That left only a single, hard truth: Getting rid of the peculiar institution was going to be a long and difficult task.

Chapter 5

FIGHTING THE GOOD FIGHT

Time passed differently for enslaved blacks and the white abolitionists who wished to help them. For the abolitionists, the long struggle for emancipation was filled with challenge, and the satisfaction of fighting for a cause. For the slaves, those years were filled with the grinding reality of sixteen-hour workdays, brutal overseers (plantation managers), and the constant fear of being sold away from family and friends.

"Sorrow and Desolation Have Their Songs"

That desperation did not always show. In fact, a casual observer might think slaves were "the most contented and happy laborers in the world," in the words of former slave Frederick Douglass. "They dance and sing, and make all manner of joyful noises . . . but it is a great mistake to suppose them happy because they sing. . . . Sorrow and desolation have their songs, as well as joy and peace."[1]

Joy and peace were rare for slaves. Their daily lives were regimented for the master's benefit, not their own. On a typical plantation, slaves lived in dirt-floor shacks, clustered together on a "slave street." The street was usually far enough from the main house so the slaves would not disturb their owners, but near enough so they always felt like the master's eye was on them. Living on the street meant getting up at the crack of dawn and working until sunset. It meant being cold in the winter, hot in the summer, and hungry most of the time.

On some plantations, slaves were allowed to have a small garden in which to grow vegetables for their own use. On others, this was considered unwise. It might encourage self-reliance, and that was the last thing the slave owners wanted. A self-reliant slave might become rebellious, and plantation society depended on black submission to white authority.

Any disobedience to that authority resulted in punishment, ranging from a quick slap for "impudence" (overly bold behavior) to the worst sort of tortures:

> My marster [master] had a barrel, with nails drove in it, then he would put you in when he couldn't think of nothin' else mean enough to do. He would put you in this barrel and roll it down a hill. When you got out you would be in a bad fix, but he didn't care. Sometimes he rolled the barrel in the river and drowned his slaves.[2]

This kind of cruelty was, fortunately, not too widespread, but it did occur—more often than the supporters of slavery would like to admit.

Whipping was the most common punishment. The weapons used ranged from thin rawhide lashes that drew blood with every stripe to broad leather straps that usually did not leave scars. Few slaves escaped the lash. Slaves remembered their worst whippings with a haunting clarity. Former slave Sarah Douglas recalled every detail of "the wors' whipping I ever got in my life":

> The last whipping Old Mis' give me she tied me to a tree and—oh, my Lord!—she whipped me that day. . . . I cried and bucked and hollered, until I couldn't. I give up for dead, and she wouldn't stop. I stop crying and said to her, "Mis', if I were you and you were me, I wouldn't beat you this way." That struck Old Mis's heart, and she let me go, and she did not have the heart to beat me anymore.[3]

The Domestic Slave Trade

For most slaves, there was one fear greater than the fear of punishment: the fear of being sold away from friends and loved ones into a new and unfamiliar environment. By the 1830s, cotton had become big business in the Deep South. Thousands of acres of it grew on plantations in Alabama, Mississippi, Georgia, and parts of Louisiana. Every one of those plantations needed a large, year-round labor force— in other words, slaves.

The Deep South needed them, and the older states of the Upper South had them. The Upper South also had depleted soil and a shaky economy. Many a Virginian or Carolinian made more money selling slaves than growing tobacco or rice. From 1830 to 1860, Virginia led this huge market, exporting nearly three hundred thousand slaves.[4]

The most sinister figure in this interstate slave trade was the slave monger (dealer). He was a middleman who bought slaves at favorable prices in the border states (the slave states of Delaware, Maryland, Kentucky, and Missouri, which shared boundaries with free states) and sold them at great profit in the Deep South. In the hands of slave mongers, people who were already regarded as property endured the added horror of becoming merchandise.

"[The slaves] are put in stalls like . . . cattle —a man and his wife with a child on each arm," said James Martin, a slave in Virginia.

> And there's a curtain, sometimes just a sheet over the front of the stall, so the bidders can't see the "stock" too soon. The overseer's standin' just outside with a big black snake whip and a . . . pistol in his belt. . . . [The overseer] makes 'em hop, he makes 'em trot, he makes 'em jump. "How much," he yells, "for this buck? A thousand? Eleven hundred? Twelve hundred dollars?" Then the bidders makes offers accordin' to size and build.[5]

Slaves could be put on the market for many reasons. Some were "surplus"—people the plantation master no longer needed on his workforce. Some were criminals, others chronic runaways or malingerers (people who pretended sickness to avoid work). Some were sold to satisfy the terms of a dead owner's will or the claims of a creditor.

Some innocently ran afoul of the wrong people. Former slave Daniel Dowdy saw his cousin put on the auction block simply because of her good looks:

> My cousin Eliza was a pretty girl. . . . Her master was her father. When the girls in the big house had beaus coming to see 'em, they'd ask, "Who is that pretty gal?" So they decided to git rid of her right away.
>
> The day they sold her will always be remembered. They stripped her to be bid off and looked at. . . . Mama and Eliza both cried when she was being showed off, and Master told 'em to shet up, before he knocked they brains out.[6]

Slaves in older, more established states, such as Virginia and Maryland, lived in terror of being "sold south" to the cotton and sugarcane fields.[7] There, the weather was steamy hot, the work punishing and endless. On long summer afternoons, many a slave keeled over in the fields. Some died of sunstroke.

The situation got so bad that outraged abolitionists claimed that Southern planters "deliberately worked their slaves to death every seven years with the intention of replacing them from profits."[8] These charges were never proven, but even Southerners admitted that conditions in the Deep South were brutal. A white Mississippian summed up the situation: "I'd ruther [sic] be dead than be a [slave] on one of these big plantations."[9]

The Quarreling Abolitionists

In 1840, the American Anti-Slavery Society came to a crossroads. On one side was the uncompromising radicalism of William Lloyd Garrison; on the other was the more conservative view represented by brothers Arthur and Lewis Tappan of New York. To Garrison, slavery was a moral issue rather than a political or economic one. Bigotry was the real enemy, and he confronted it with characteristic zeal. He invited both black people and women to join the Anti-Slavery Society as full members. They could participate freely in discussions, hold office within the organization, and represent the society as lecturers.

Garrison did not stop there. He called on the society's members to withdraw from any political, religious, or social organization that would not declare slavery a sin against humankind. This included the government of the

United States and most religious denominations. Many members thought he was going too far; they were not ready to renounce their churches or abandon politics—and they were certainly not ready to accept blacks and women as equals. Abolitionists were not saints or angels. They were human beings who shared the common prejudices of their day—sexism and racism included. Within the movement there were those who insisted that a woman's place was in the home, and those who believed that black people were inferior to whites.

Garrison refused to compromise, believing that to do so would be nothing less than a sin against God and humanity. At the 1840 convention, he forced a vote that placed Quaker feminist Abby Kelley on the business committee. The opposition balked at the prospect of a woman in what they considered a man's job. About three hundred men staged a walkout. They held a separate meeting to form a new organization: the American and Foreign Anti-Slavery Society. One of their first acts was to forbid women to vote or hold office in the group.

With a single stroke, the Garrisonians had become the "old org" (slang for "old organization") of a divided movement.[10] The rival "new org" formed a political party called the Liberty party and planned to make its voice heard in the government.

The old org continued with its moral persuasion and radical philosophies. William Lloyd Garrison's active recruitment of blacks and women launched the public careers of groundbreakers like Abby Kelley, Frederick Douglass, and Sojourner Truth.

A Public-Speaking Woman

Abby Kelley was one of the first women to play a leadership role in the Anti-Slavery Society. It was her passion for the cause that brought women like Lucy Stone and Susan B. Anthony into the movement.

The daughter of a Quaker farm family, Abby Kelley grew up as something of a tomboy. She left dolls and domesticity to her sisters, preferring to study or to follow her father around the farm, helping with the daily chores. From her pious mother, she learned about the "inner light" of Quaker tradition. According to the Quakers, this light was the spirit of God living within a person. Every living soul had a piece of it, and every Christian had a duty to follow wherever it might lead.

Abby Kelley's light led to William Lloyd Garrison and the abolition movement. In 1836, she joined the Female Anti-Slavery Society. In 1839, she took to the lecture circuit, to the dismay of those who believed a woman's place was in the home. Kelley's presence on the speaker's platform scandalized upright, respectable folks:

> Ministers preached against her, calling her "a very bad woman," a "Jezebel" sent by Satan to entice and destroy. Politicians [called] her a "man woman"; newspapers labeled her "infidel" or "Communist." During two decades of public speaking she dodged rotten eggs, rum bottles, and the contents of outhouses.[11]

In spite of it all, Abby Kelley would not quit. She was sustained by her Quaker faith, a belief in the rightness of her cause, and a wit sharp enough to get the best of many a heckler. At one of her lectures, a man in the audience leapt to his feet and tried to argue that slavery was a natural and normal part of human society. By way of proof, he appealed to history: "'When did slavery [begin]?' he demanded. 'How long has it existed?'" Abby Kelley did not miss a beat: "'About as long as murder,'" she replied.[12] The audience burst into applause.

The "Lion" of the Abolition Movement

Frederick Douglass, born a slave in 1817 or 1818, was tall and handsome, with a quick mind and a commanding presence. After escaping slavery in 1838, he made his way to the North, eventually settling in New Bedford, Massachusetts.

William Lloyd Garrison first heard him speak at an antislavery convention in August 1841. Garrison described the occasion in the preface he wrote for Frederick Douglass's autobiography, *Narrative of the Life of Frederick Douglass, an American Slave*:

> It was at once deeply impressed upon my mind, that, if Mr. Douglass could be persuaded to consecrate his time and talents to the promotion of the anti-slavery enterprise, a powerful [force] would be given to it, and a stunning blow . . . inflicted on northern prejudice against a colored complexion.[13]

Garrison was right. Frederick Douglass could speak and write about slavery with the sure touch of experience. Having been held in slavery himself, he could speak about freedom with a passion that matched anything the Founding Fathers of the American Revolution had produced.

Douglass's description of his first childhood awareness of freedom is one of the most impressive and memorable passages in the *Narrative*:

Freedom now appeared, to disappear no more forever. It was heard in every sound, and seen in every thing. It was ever present to torment me with a sense of my wretched condition. I saw nothing without seeing it, I heard nothing without hearing it, and felt nothing without feeling it. It looked from every star, it smiled in every calm, breathed in every wind, and moved in every storm.[14]

Garrison recruited Douglass to the cause of abolition, and thus became the mentor (teacher or guide) of the man who would become the most famous African American of his time. Over a span of years, the student would come to outshine the teacher in the minds and hearts of the public.

If Garrison was jealous of Douglass's popularity, he hid it for the benefit of the abolitionist cause. As Douglass biographer William S. McFeely put it, Garrison knew that "no one better exemplified that sacred cause than the magnificent slave."[15]

Isabella, Called Sojourner Truth

The slave child Isabella was born sometime in the late 1790s. Nobody knows the hour, the day, or even the year. The legendary abolitionist Sojourner Truth was "born" on June 1, 1843. On that day, Isabella recreated herself as Sojourner Truth. She mixed parts of her own past with the history of her people, and added a vibrant religious faith.

The result was a public personality of strength, wit, and conviction. Sojourner Truth stood almost six feet tall. On the platform she was part preacher, part teacher, part performer. She moved back and forth between speaking and singing with ease.

Her husky contralto voice was untrained but powerful. She sang about death and redemption, about faith, love, and freedom. One of her favorites was a resurrection hymn:

> *It was early in the morning—it was early in the morning,*
> *Just at the break of day—*
> *When he rose—when he rose—when he rose,*
> *And went to heaven on a cloud.*[16]

She first appeared on the national abolitionist scene in May 1845, when she addressed the annual meeting of William Lloyd Garrison's old org faithful. A newspaper report on the speech did not even mention her name. It said only that "a woman who had been a slave, but more recently resident of Northampton, Mass." had spoken at the meeting with "good sense and strong feeling."[17]

Garrison recognized Truth's spellbinding effect on audiences. By 1851, he had recruited her to go on the lecture circuit. She shared the podium with many of the leading abolitionists of her day, becoming a symbol of the strong black woman who had faced the worst slavery had to offer and emerged victorious.

Black people like Sojourner Truth and Frederick Douglass contributed to the cause not only by what they did but by who they were. Their obvious talent caused many white people to take a serious look at their assumptions about race and ability.

Chapter 6

TRAVELING THE FREEDOM ROAD

Opponents of slavery did not stop with literature and lectures. Some abolitionists offered more personal—and much more risky—help. There were lawyers who defended black people in court, private citizens who bought the freedom of slaves they scarcely knew, and Underground Railroad operatives who smuggled escaping slaves to safety in the North.

Finally, there were the slaves themselves: black people who held on to their human dignity in spite of slavery, those who risked everything to run away, and those who placed themselves in danger to help others run away.

The Strange Affair of the *Amistad*

In August 1839, a black-hulled schooner appeared off the coast of Long Island, New York. No flag flew from its mast to reveal its point of origin. Its sails were shredded, its decks littered with garbage. Wherever this ship had come from, its voyage had not been an easy one.

The ship was the *Amistad* (Spanish for "friendship"), a Spanish slaver out of Cuba. On board were thirty-nine

African men, four African children, two terrified Spaniards, and a teenage slave named Antonio. American officials soon faced a dilemma. The Africans had risen up against the Spaniards, killing all but two of them; this much was certain. The rest was unclear.

If the black people were Cuban slaves, as the Spaniards claimed, then they were guilty of mutiny and should be returned to the proper authorities. If they were kidnapped Africans, then they were free men resisting unlawful captivity. (Spain had formally outlawed the international slave trade in 1820.)

Antislavery activists in New York saw the case as a chance to strike a blow for abolition. Controversy swirled around it, and even pro-slavery people were uncertain about the true status of these prisoners. In the midst of the growing controversy was the intriguing figure of Cinqué, leader of the *Amistad* blacks.

In appearance and conduct, he was an appealing figure: a man of "fine proportions," who possessed a "good degree of gracefulness and native dignity," according to New York abolitionist Lewis Tappan.[1]

The case of the *Amistad* prisoners went all the way to the United States Supreme Court, where former president John Quincy Adams argued for the Africans. On March 9, 1841, the Court ruled in favor of the defendants. They were not slaves, but kidnapped Africans, who "had the . . . right of self-defense and could kill their captors to win freedom."[2]

Cinqué and the surviving Africans were free to return to their homes. The boy Antonio was not so fortunate; he actually was a slave, property of the late captain of the *Amistad*. As such, he was returned to Cuba. Thus, the

Court affirmed the legality of slavery with one hand, and dispensed "color-blind" justice with the other.

According to historian Howard Jones, the importance of the *Amistad* case

> lies not so much in the reasoning behind the Supreme Court's decision but in the fact that the blacks, in collaboration with white abolitionists, had won freedom. Legal technicalities did not matter. . . . [T]he popular impression of blacks liberated from slavery spoke much more loudly than did the legal limitations of the decision. . . . In that sense the *Amistad* case made a significant contribution to the fight against slavery.[3]

The Underground Railroad

The Underground Railroad, a network of escape routes and safe houses for runaway slaves, is one of the most legendary operations in American history. People of conscience, both white and black, helped escaping slaves cross to freedom in the North.

Because the operation was surrounded by secrecy, many of the facts about its day-to-day workings are not clear. The Underground Railroad has, therefore, become a thing of myth and mystery, complete with heroes and villains, grand adventures, narrow escapes, and its own special language:

> The houses where aid and shelter were given were known as "stations"; those in charge of the "stations" were "station-masters" or "agents"; those in charge of sending fugitives to "stations" were "brakemen"; and "conductors" guided the slaves from station to station. People who contributed money, clothing, and other financial support to the venture were "stockholders." The fugitives were . . .

"valuable pieces of ebony," a "bale of Southern goods," or "prime articles"—in short, anything but slaves.[4]

The work was both dangerous and illegal, so it attracted people who were dedicated, daring, and often unconventional. The borderlands between the free states of the North and the slave states of the South were hotbeds of Underground Railroad activity. Two especially daring groups operated in Cincinnati and Ripley, on the banks of the Ohio River.

The Cincinnati group was headed by Levi Coffin, a Quaker with a reputation for imaginative rescues. Coffin once smuggled more than twenty escaped slaves to safety by disguising them as mourners in a funeral procession. He hired a hearse for the "body" and black-curtained carriages for all the "mourners." Late in the night, on the outskirts of Cincinnati, the solemn procession began. By the time it reached its destination, the mourners had disappeared.

Upriver in Ripley, the operation was headed by John Rankin, a minister who had been run out of Kentucky for his abolitionist views. John Parker, a former slave who became one of the best Underground Railroad conductors on the river, credited Rankin and his six sons with keeping the Underground unit together. The Rankin house was

> perched on [a] high hill behind the town. . . . A lighted candle stood as a beacon which could be seen from across the river, and like the north star was the guide to the fleeing slave. In this eagle's nest, Rev. John Rankin and his sons held forth during many stormy years, and only left the old home when their work was well and lastingly done.[5]

John Parker led a double life for nearly fifteen years. By day, he worked as an iron molder. By night, he smuggled slaves across the river from Kentucky. With every run, he took a terrible risk. He could be gunned down by slave catchers or betrayed by the very people he was trying to help. If he got caught, the government would take away all his property and send him to prison.

Even the thought of punishment did not stop John Parker. He remembered the horrors of slavery too well to turn his back on fugitives whose only crime was wanting to be free. On many a dark night, Parker paddled his skiff across the river to the Kentucky shore, returning with slaves on their way to freedom. When John Parker died in 1900, the Cincinnati *Commercial Tribune* noted that "a more fearless creature never lived. He gloried in danger. . . . He would go boldly over into the enemy's camp and [lead] the fugitives to freedom."[6]

The Saga of Harriet Tubman

Of all the conductors on the Underground Railroad, perhaps the most famous was Harriet Tubman. Born a slave in Maryland in 1820 or 1821, the child called Araminta was all the things a slave should not be: strong-willed, independent, and outspoken. These qualities got her into trouble more than once.

As a youngster, she got so many whippings that she learned to protect herself with extra layers of clothes, then scream and cry as if every blow were hitting its mark. In 1849, she ran away from the plantation, heading north to freedom. She returned south the first time to find her husband, John Tubman, a free black living in Cambridge, Maryland. He had already taken another wife and had no desire to leave his reasonably comfortable situation. Harriet Tubman never saw him again. Out of her grief at this betrayal, she "determined to give her life to brave deeds . . . and with her simple brave motto, 'I can't die but once,' she began the work which has made her Moses—the deliverer of her people."[7]

Moving by night, she became expert at slipping past patrols and organizing escapes. Slaveholders offered a forty-thousand-dollar reward for her capture. No one ever got to claim it. During the Civil War, Tubman worked as a spy for the Union Army, going behind enemy lines to gather valuable information about Confederate troop strength and battle plans. When the war ended, she settled in Auburn, New York, where she remained until her death in 1913.[8]

Adventures in Freedom

Not everyone who escaped slavery had the help of a big organization. Many did it entirely on their own or with the help of a few trusted friends. Even those who did get help from the Underground Railroad usually had to begin the journey on their own. There was no organized rescue network in the Deep South. Conductor John Parker pointed this out in his auto-biography:

> Men and women whom I helped on their way came from Tennessee, requiring weeks to make the journey, sleeping under the trees in the daytime and slowly picking their dangerous way at night. How they crossed the numerous creeks that lay waiting for them like a trap was unbelievable to me. As a matter of fact, they became backwoodsmen, following the north star, or even mountains, to reach their destination, the Ohio River. . . . These long-distance travelers were usually people strong physically, as well as

people of character, and were resourceful when confronted with trouble, otherwise they could have never escaped.[9]

Henry Brown of Virginia made one of the most original escapes ever recorded. He had himself nailed into a wooden box and shipped to Philadelphia. Despite the marking "this side up with care," Brown spent a good many hours on his head in an overland express baggage car. Members of the Philadelphia Vigilance Committee had been alerted to expect a very unusual shipment. When it arrived, they opened the crate and out popped a bedraggled but happy Henry Brown. From that moment on, he became known as Box Brown, and his story both inspired and amused everyone who heard it.

An Unpopular War

Conflicts over slavery arose every time Americans began to settle new territories. Would these territories be slave or free? Who would decide? These questions were in the back of many people's minds when the United States declared war on Mexico in May 1846.

As justification for the war, the United States government claimed Mexico had invaded American territory. Actually, the territory in question was a matter of dispute between the two governments. When the United States annexed Texas as a state, it set the southwest boundary at the Rio Grande. Mexico claimed that the boundary should be the Nueces River, some one hundred miles east of the Rio Grande.

The United States sent troops into the disputed area on January 13, 1846. By May 8, the Mexicans had responded with troops of their own. The resulting battle gave President James K. Polk the excuse he needed to ask

Congress for a declaration of war: "Mexico has passed the boundary of the United States," Polk said in his message to Congress, "has invaded our territory and shed American blood upon American soil. War exists, and, notwithstanding all our effort to avoid it, exists by the act of Mexico herself."[10]

In spite of the speech-making, many Americans felt that the war against Mexico was nothing but a thinly disguised grab for territory. Many Southerners hailed it openly as an opportunity to extend the territory of slavery and "widen the field of Southern enterprise and power in the future."[11]

Northern antiwar sentiment was spearheaded by the abolitionists. People such as poet James Russell Lowell and minister Theodore Parker rallied to the cause, and first-term Illinois Congressman Abraham Lincoln called President Polk's attempt to portray Mexico as the aggressor "the sheerest deception."[12]

Writer Henry David Thoreau protested through an act of civil disobedience. He spent a night in jail for refusing to pay his poll tax. "Under a government which imprisons unjustly, the true place for a just man is also a prison," he wrote in "Civil Disobedience," the essay that set forth his principles of nonviolent resistance to unjust laws:

> It is [in prison] that the fugitive slave, and the Mexican prisoner on parole, and the Indian come to plead the wrongs of his race should find [men of justice]; on that separate but more free and honorable ground, where the state places those who are not *with* her, but *against* her,— the only house in a slave-state in which a free man can abide with honor.[13]

The United States won the war with Mexico in convincing fashion. On February 2, 1848, the Treaty of Guadalupe-Hidalgo established the border of Texas at the Rio Grande and stripped Mexico of lands that included all of the present states of California and New Mexico, along with parts of Nevada, Utah, Arizona, Colorado, and Wyoming.

Southerners saw an opportunity to take their way of life into new territories. Northerners disagreed. Even those who were not involved in the abolitionist cause had no desire to see the spread of a slavery-based economy: "We are no abolitionists in the popular sense of the term," noted the Cincinnati *Daily Unionist*, "but we would belie our convictions of democracy if we did not oppose slavery's expansion over new lands."[14]

This attitude was becoming typical in the free states. Opposition to the expansion of slavery grew out of many concerns—some political, some economic, some social, and some racial. More slave states meant more pro-slavery legislators in Congress and more pro-slavery control over the national government. Northerners had other ideas about what America's future ought to be. "Northern farmers wanted western lands for their own use as homesteads," wrote historian Bruce Levine,

> and many urban working people shared [that] dream. . . . Neither [group] wished to dwell among slaves, compete with slave labor, or be governed locally by slave-owning politicians. Even [people] who expected to remain in the East wanted the West guaranteed as "free soil" for the future benefit of neighbors, children, grandchildren, and future immigrants.[15]

As Free-Soil Northerners joined with abolitionists to oppose the spread of slavery, they put pressure on Washington politicians and Southern apologists (people who argue for a cause) for slavery. Once more, the issue was the expansion of slavery into new territories, and once more the leaders of the country would try to patch together an agreement that would preserve the Union.

Chapter 7

THE CONFLICT DEEPENS

After the Mexican War, there was a new urgency in the South's struggle to maintain a slave society. Simple survival was no longer enough; the peculiar institution needed to grow. If abolitionists and Free-Soilers succeeded in isolating slavery behind ever-shrinking borders, the Southern way of life would eventually wither away and die.

The legal and ideological struggles that began after the Mexican War had their foundations in one great, underlying conflict: The South wanted to protect slavery and preserve Southern culture; the North wanted to stop the expansion of slavery and preserve the Union.

The Compromise of 1850

The debate on the status of slavery in the former Mexican territories began even before the war was won. In the summer of 1846, Congressman David Wilmot of Pennsylvania proposed legislation that would permanently outlaw slavery in any and all territories acquired from Mexico. Southerners were outraged.

In 1849, California's petition to enter the Union as a free state helped bring the matter to a head. In order to act on California's petition, Congress had to deal with the whole question of slavery in the new territories. Though supporters of the Wilmot Proviso, as Congressman Wilmot's legislation was called, agreed that a complete prohibition of slavery was not workable, they did not agree on what sort of compromise might hold the Union together.

President James K. Polk favored a formal extension of the Missouri Compromise line of 36°30' all the way to the Pacific Ocean. John C. Calhoun, a South Carolina slaveholder and senator, wanted the national government to guarantee the property rights of all slaveholders who settled anywhere in the new territories. Vice President George Dallas called for popular sovereignty, which was perhaps the simplest solution of all: Let the people of each new territory decide the matter for themselves.

The result of all this maneuvering was anything but simple. In the end, a series of five pieces of legislation made up the Compromise of 1850. Three dealt directly with the lands acquired from Mexico: California was accepted into the Union with a state constitution that outlawed slavery, while New Mexico and Utah were chartered as territories with the issue of slavery to be decided by popular sovereignty.

The last two resolutions tried to give each side something it wanted. For the abolitionists, Congress outlawed the slave trade in Washington, D.C. For the slaveholders, it passed a new, stronger Fugitive Slave Law. There had been a fugitive law, designed to help slave owners recover runaway slaves, on the books since 1793, but Northerners largely ignored it. Some states had even passed "personal freedom" laws to protect runaway slaves from the law.

The new law had teeth. It increased penalties for aiding fugitive slaves in any way. It also allowed federal marshals to draft local citizens into posses and force them to help track down the slaves who had run away from bondage.

Slaveholders hoped this law would discourage new escapes, give abolitionists second thoughts about helping runaways, and force earlier escapees into hiding. When the law went into effect, blacks living in the North without freedom papers flooded into Canada. Some escapees had lived free for years. They had jobs, homes, families, and the feeling that slavery was well behind them. The new law stripped away that feeling. In its place was the old fear of bondage.

Acts of Open Defiance

As Southerners tried to enforce their property rights in the North, they ran into an unexpected backlash. Northern people who had dismissed slavery as a Southern problem suddenly could not do that anymore. The Fugitive Slave Law brought it right into their own backyards. It was one thing to know that slavery existed down in Georgia or Mississippi or Louisiana. It was quite another thing to hunt down terrified runaways and send them back into bondage.

In a nation where freedom was the watchword, that just did not seem right. Sympathy for the escapees ran high, and the old Southern arguments about slaves being well treated and happy did not ring true.

Abolitionists and their supporters openly defied the Fugitive Slave Law. In Lancaster County, Pennsylvania, ordinarily peaceable Quakers rioted when a federal marshal ordered them to help catch a runaway slave. In Boston, a group of African Americans stormed the jail to rescue a captive slave from government authorities and send him on his way to Canada.

Some years later, Boston became the scene of a fugitive deportation that might have been comical if the consequences had not been so serious. The episode began with the arrest of Anthony Burns, an escaped slave from Virginia. Militant clergyman Thomas Wentworth Higginson led an attack on the jail to rescue Burns. The attempt failed, but not before a deputy was killed in the fighting.

An angered President Franklin Pierce pulled out all the stops to enforce the Fugitive Slave Law in this controversial case. He dispatched more than a thousand troops to Boston to make sure that Anthony Burns would be sent back to Virginia, as provided by law. On the day federal marshals marched the prisoner from the courthouse to a waiting ship, fifty thousand people lined the way, hissing and shouting. Flags flew at half mast, and buildings were draped in mourning black. All over Massachusetts, church bells tolled and dummies of President Pierce burned in effigy.

These public displays of sympathy could not save Anthony Burns, but they did make certain that the government paid a high price for sending him back into bondage. According to some estimates, the cost of arresting, guarding, and transporting this one escaped slave came to a whopping one hundred thousand dollars.[1]

The Saga of *Uncle Tom's Cabin*

In 1852, when public resentment for the Fugitive Slave Law was deepening the gulf between North and South, a controversial book appeared on the scene. *Uncle Tom's Cabin* by Harriet Beecher Stowe captured the imagination, and the conscience, of the nation. This was no learned analysis of the problem of human bondage. This was a *story*, a work of fiction that presented black people as human beings who loved, laughed, suffered, and died just like all other human beings.

In its first year, *Uncle Tom's Cabin* sold 1.2 million copies, becoming one of the best-selling novels of its day.[2] It was also made into a play that attracted large and sympathetic audiences.

Uncle Tom's Cabin contains one of the most famous scenes in literature: Eliza on the ice. The slave Eliza, having learned that her child is to be sold, escapes across the breaking ice of the Ohio River, jumping from shard to shard with the baby in her arms.

Eliza and her child are saved by this desperately courageous act. By contrast, the elderly slave Tom, who remains unfailingly obedient to his white masters, is finally beaten to death by the sadistic Simon Legree.

In an article, literary critic Andrew Delbanco noted that both Eliza's and Tom's stories are written in a melodramatic (sensationalized, highly emotional) style. "They are shrieks more than arguments," he said, and added a telling observation from past reviewers: "it has been said that *Uncle Tom's Cabin* was written in tears rather than in ink."[3]

There is a story that President Abraham Lincoln once described Harriet Beecher Stowe as "the little woman who wrote the book that started this great war [the Civil War]."[4] The story may not be factual, but it does capture an important truth: *Uncle Tom's Cabin* changed people's thinking. It was quite likely the most powerful piece of antislavery literature ever written.

Bleeding Kansas

In 1854, passage of the Kansas-Nebraska Act ended another long battle in Congress, and began a new, bloodier one on the frontier. This controversial law first divided the Kansas frontier into two territories—Kansas and Nebraska—then gave settlers the right to decide the slavery issue for themselves.

The act destroyed the Missouri Compromise. Under its terms, both Kansas and Nebraska should have become free states because they were north of the 36°30' line. In passing the Kansas-Nebraska Act, Congress threw out the law that had kept the peace for thirty-four years.

In the North, there was outrage; in the South, rejoicing. In Kansas there was violence, as both sides in the argument over slavery sought to gain the upper hand. By 1855, there were two competing governments in Kansas, each pressing its claim to legitimacy. There were also two fighting groups: the so-called Border Ruffians, who slipped in from Missouri to back the pro-slavery cause, and the Jayhawkers, who supported the Free-Soilers.[5]

Both sides committed atrocities against each other. There were murders, bushwhackings (surprise attacks), and burnings. *New York Tribune* editor Horace Greeley coined the term that would forever describe the territory during those violent years: *Bleeding Kansas.*[6]

It was in Bleeding Kansas that the fanatical abolitionist John Brown first made his mark. As the founder and commander of a militia called the Liberty Guards, he became known as a bold and ruthless fighter for the antislavery cause.

The Liberty Guards "terrorized the Missouri-Kansas border," staging surprise attacks on every pro-slavery camp or settlement they could find.[7] One such raid became known as the Pottawatomie Massacre. It grew out of Brown's rage when a pro-slavery gang sacked and

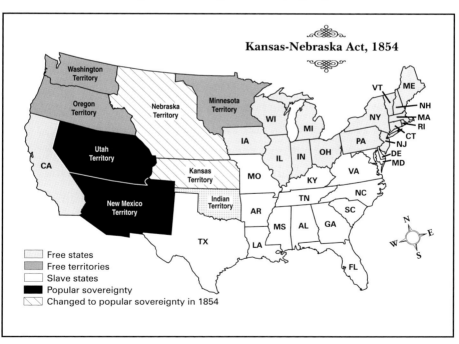

In 1854, Congress passed the Kansas-Nebraska Act, allowing popular sovereignty to decide whether the new territories would be slave or free. The result was war between pro-slavery and antislavery forces.

burned the town of Lawrence, Kansas, in May 1856. Brown's Guards rounded up the five pro-slavery men they considered most responsible for the attack and killed them on the banks of the Pottawatomie River.

Four months later, Brown's son Frederick was killed in a raid on the settlement of Osawatomie. As the grieving father mourned his son, he also renewed his vow to destroy the institution of slavery. "I have only a short time to live—only one death to die," he said, "and I will die fighting for this cause."[8] By the end of the decade, those words would prove prophetic.

Politics and Abolition

Passage of the Kansas-Nebraska Act caused a political crisis that resulted in the downfall of the political party known as the Whigs. The party began in the 1830s to oppose the policies of President Andrew Jackson. Jacksonian Democrats favored rule by the common people and a relatively weak national government. The Whigs wanted a strong national government that could implement an aggressive program of economic expansion. The Whig party attracted a broad base of support, including Northern industrialists and shopkeepers, Southern agricultural interests, and moralists who wanted a national program of social, as well as economic, reform.

In the election of 1840, the Whigs ran an aggressive campaign filled with slogans, songs, rallies, and parades. Riding an economic downturn and using the famous catchphrase "Tippecanoe and Tyler Too," the Whigs elected their first president, John Tyler, who served from 1841 to 1845.

After the war with Mexico brought new territories under United States control, rifts began to appear in the Whig party. Southern Whigs supported the expansion of slavery into the new territories; Northern Whigs opposed it.

After passage of the Kansas-Nebraska Act, the Northern faction sided with political abolitionists such as the Liberty party and the Free-Soil party. On March 20, 1854, this coalition (alliance) gathered at Ripon, Wisconsin, to create a new political force: the Republican party.

In 1856, they nominated their first candidate for president—explorer, military hero, and former senator from California John C. Frémont. Though Frémont lost to Democrat James Buchanan, his party had established itself as an important political force.

The Case of Dred Scott, a Slave

While the Republican party was gaining strength between 1856 and 1860, the abolitionist cause suffered a major setback. On March 6, 1857, the United States Supreme Court delivered what has been called "the most infamous ruling [it] ever rendered."[9] The facts of the case were fairly simple: A slave named Dred Scott sued for his freedom on the grounds that he had lived in the free state of Illinois and the free territory of Wisconsin for five years.

The case was filed in the slave state of Missouri, after Scott returned there with his owner. In 1850, a St. Louis jury found for Scott, but the verdict was overturned in 1852 by the Missouri Supreme Court, which ruled that living in free territory did not make Dred Scott a free man.

Scott and his attorneys put this ruling to the test in the United States Supreme Court. The results of that action shook the antislavery movement to its very foundations.

The highest court in the land said that Dred Scott was still a slave, no matter how long he had lived in free territory. In the majority opinion, Chief Justice Roger B. Taney declared that black people were "considered as a subordinate and inferior class of beings," by the Framers of the Constitution.[10]

Africans and their descendants were, therefore, "not included, and were not intended to be included, under the word 'citizens' in the Constitution." Whether slave or free, they "had no rights which the white man was bound to respect."[11]

In this same opinion, the Court stripped Congress of the authority to forbid slavery in United States territories: "no word can be found in the Constitution which gives Congress a greater power over slave property . . . than property of any other description," wrote Chief Justice Taney.

On the basis of this finding, the Court ruled that "the act of Congress which prohibited a citizen from owning [slaves] in the territory of the United States north of the [Missouri Compromise] line . . . is not warranted by the Constitution, and is therefore void."[12]

By the time this ruling came down, the 36°30' line had already been breached. Therefore, the decision of the Court did not affect the Missouri Compromise. Instead, it set a precedent (a guide for future actions), putting Congress on notice that similar laws to control the spread of slavery would be struck down as unconstitutional.

The ruling sent shock waves through the antislavery community, delighted the slaveholding South, and placed western settlers on notice that they would have to solve the slavery issue for themselves.

John Brown's Raid

In the autumn after the *Dred Scott* ruling, John Brown began recruiting a guerrilla force for an ambitious military operation. He intended to find a defensible spot in the mountains, where he could set up a base from which to launch raids against slave plantations. Liberated slaves would then flock to his banner and join the fight for freedom; of this, Brown felt certain. And he would lead them to victory.

Brown's first target was the federal arsenal at Harpers Ferry, Virginia (present-day West Virginia). Brown planned to take the arsenal with a single, fierce strike and use its weapons to arm liberated slaves for the coming battle against the peculiar institution.

It was a grandiose (showy, overdone) plan, but John Brown was able to convince a number of influential abolitionists that it could work. His financial backers included such prominent men as Boston educator Samuel Gridley Howe, former New York Congressman Gerrit Smith, and Thomas Wentworth Higginson, the clergyman who had opposed the Fugitive Slave Law by trying to rescue Anthony Burns.

Brown attacked Harpers Ferry on October 16, 1859, with a hand-picked force of twenty-one men, whom he called the "Provisional Army of the United States."[13] They entered silently in the dead of night, crossing the Baltimore and Ohio Railroad bridge into Harpers Ferry. Two men stayed behind to block off the bridge so that no railroad traffic could pass without Brown's knowledge and consent.

The main force made straight for the armory, where they easily overpowered the night watchman and set up a temporary headquarters. From there, Brown sent groups of his men to take care of various objectives, including occupying a nearby rifle factory, standing guard at the Shenandoah River bridge, and gathering important citizens as hostages.

The takeover went smoothly in the darkness. At daybreak, the situation quickly changed. When the locals realized what had happened, a crowd of armed and angry citizens gathered in front of the armory. By noon, help had arrived in the form of two militias from neighboring towns. Other units soon followed. Militias came from Shepherdstown and Winchester in Virginia, and from Frederick and Baltimore in Maryland. A company of United States Marines led by Colonel Robert E. Lee arrived around eleven o'clock that night.

John Brown was probably the only person in Harpers Ferry who still believed his ragtag little army could prevail. Lee's marines attacked in the early morning, making short work of Brown's abolitionist forces. John Brown was captured alive but wounded, along with four of his men. Seven had escaped. The rest were dead.

Brown stood trial for his crimes and was sentenced to hang. On December 2, 1859, he died on the gallows in Charles Town, Virginia. His memory, however, lived on. In the North, it sparked new militancy; in the South, new fears.

The raid on Harpers Ferry was a turning point in the long struggle against slavery. Even though it failed, it put the slave states on notice that the time for talk was almost over.

Chapter 8

WAR AND ABOLITION

The 1860 presidential campaign was a collision of factions trying to establish their positions on slavery. Americans seemed to sense the importance of this campaign. Speeches, debates, rallies, and informal discussions centered on the coming election and how it would affect the fate of the nation. The interest went beyond race and gender; slaves and women could not vote, yet they, too, followed and discussed the campaign.

From Compromise to Confrontation

In April 1860, Democrats gathered at Charleston, South Carolina, for their national convention. The Northern and Southern branches of the party were unable to develop a party platform that would satisfy both of them. Southern delegates wanted to commit the party to federal protection of slavery, both in the South itself and in the territories. They also wanted veto power over the party's selection of a presidential candidate, which the Northern delegates refused to give them.

The issues split the party. In separate conventions, the Northern group nominated Stephen A. Douglas for president; while the Southerners nominated John C. Breckinridge, a prominent slaveholder from Kentucky.

The new Constitutional Union party grew out of the desperate desire to save the Union at all costs. Compromise and unity were its watchwords; it had no platform as such, only a vow "to recognize no political principle other than the Constitution of the Country, the Union of the States, and the Enforcement of the Laws."[1] The party nominated Tennessee slaveholder John Bell for president and Harvard University president Edward Everett for vice president.

The Republicans nominated Abraham Lincoln of Illinois, a man known for his homespun wisdom and good common sense. Lincoln was not an abolitionist. Though he personally thought slavery was wrong, he publicly opposed only its expansion, not its existence. He took great pains to state that he had "no purpose, directly or indirectly, to interfere with the institution of slavery in the State where it exists."[2]

In spite of these assurances, the South regarded Abraham Lincoln as the antislavery candidate of an antislavery party. When he won the 1860 election, Southerners knew they had lost control of the government. The North had sent a message, loud and clear: The days of making deals were over. As one disappointed supporter of Stephen A. Douglas put it, "No compromise on earth can ever unite the cotton states with the old Union."[3]

On December 20, 1860, barely a month after Abraham Lincoln's election, South Carolina seceded from (left) the Union. Six other states of the Deep South soon followed. In February 1861, the new Confederate States of America was established at a convention in Montgomery, Alabama. The delegates created a constitution, named a temporary congress, and chose Jefferson Davis, a Mississippi planter and former senator, as their temporary president.

In his inaugural address of March 4, 1861, President Lincoln made it clear that secession would not be tolerated: "no State upon its own . . . can lawfully get out of the Union," he said.[4] Therefore, "resolves and ordinances to that effect are legally void; and that acts of violence, within any State or States, against the authority of the United States, are insurrectionary or revolutionary, according to circumstances."[5]

The line in the sand was drawn.

In the predawn hours of April 12, 1861, Confederate gunners opened fire on Fort Sumter, South Carolina, beginning what would become the deadliest war in American history.

The Fight for Freedom

The Civil War began as a fight to preserve the Union, and became a fight to free the slaves. Abolitionists and free blacks pressed the cause in the North; enslaved blacks pressed it in the South. "The American people . . . may refuse to recognize it for a time," Frederick Douglass once said, "but the 'inexorable logic of events' will force it upon them in the end; that the war now being waged in this land is a war for and against slavery."[6]

Douglass was right. Slowly, over time and in small ways, the emphasis shifted. For example, at the beginning of the war, field commanders had standing orders to return escaped slaves to their masters. No congressional ruling or presidential decree ended that practice; General

Benjamin Butler did it in the field, on his own authority. He was in command when three escaped slaves asked for sanctuary at Fort Monroe, Virginia. Apart from the moral considerations, Butler thought it would be pure foolishness to return these men to their masters. They would only be forced to work for the Confederacy. Why shouldn't they be allowed to work for the Union? Butler promptly declared the three refugees "contraband of war."[7]

It was an ingenious solution. Butler used the law that made these people into property to justify not returning them to their masters. In time of war, contraband, or illegal, property could be seized in order to keep it out of enemy hands. Butler gave the escapees sanctuary and offered them jobs in the fort's supply office. They accepted gladly. The name "contrabands" stuck, and so did the practice of using liberated or escaped slaves as workers and later as soldiers for the cause of freedom.

Emancipation!

On January 1, 1863, President Lincoln issued the Emancipation Proclamation. This document would change the focus of the Civil War and the course of American history. It read: "I do order and declare that all persons held as slaves within . . . designated States and parts of States are, and henceforward shall be, free. . . ."[8]

"I never saw Joy before," Frederick Douglass said, recalling the gathering in Boston where he awaited news that the Emancipation Proclamation had been signed. When the announcement came,

> Men, women, young and old, were up; hats and bonnets were in the air. . . . There was shouting and singing, "Glory Hallelujah," "Old John Brown," "Marching On,"

and "Blow Ye, the Trumpet Blow!"—till we got up such a state of enthusiasm that almost anything seemed witty—and entirely appropriate to the glorious occasion.[9]

For political reasons, the Emancipation Proclamation did not include slaves in states that had remained loyal to the Union. The border states of Maryland, Delaware, Kentucky, Missouri, and the new breakaway state of West Virginia had legal slavery, yet did not secede from the Union. Lincoln could not risk losing them to the Confederacy.

The president's action reassured abolitionists that the end of slavery had become "a basic war goal and a virtual certainty."[10] It also opened the door for black people to take an official role in the struggle for their freedom.

Lincoln pledged that freed slaves and other African Americans would be "received into the armed service of the United States to garrison forts, positions, stations, and other places, and to man vessels of all sorts in said service."[11]

The Fighting 54th

Just weeks after President Lincoln opened the door for African Americans to serve in the military, the 54th Massachusetts Infantry became the first black regiment in the Union Army. It was formed out of the faith of white abolitionists, the courage of black freedmen, and the determination of military and government leaders who believed they could turn slaves into soldiers.

When Massachusetts Governor John A. Andrew organized the 54th, he staked his political career and personal reputation on its success. Many thought he had taken leave of his senses. A regiment of black soldiers?

It would never work, they said, and they gave a host of reasons:

> blacks would not enlist; blacks were too cowardly to fight and would run when faced with white Southerners; blacks were not intelligent enough to learn drill; blacks with guns would return to the savage instincts of the jungle . . . blacks would demoralize white soldiers.[12]

In what was perhaps a concession to the racism of the day, Andrew made it clear that the officers of the 54th would be white. To command the regiment, he chose twenty-six-year-old Robert Gould Shaw. Shaw was a captain in the 2nd Massachusetts Infantry. He was also the

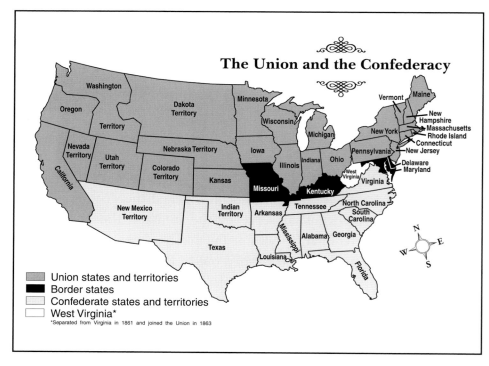

A map of how the United States was divided during the Civil War. At first, to avoid losing the loyalty of the border states, the Emancipation Proclamation applied only to the states in that had seceded.

son of a prominent and wealthy Boston family with excellent credentials in the abolition movement. The governor offered him a promotion to colonel and a chance to make history.

Shaw accepted the challenge, but not without deep misgivings. Abolitionist or not, he had his own doubts about the abilities of African Americans. He soon learned that those doubts were unfounded. The men learned quickly and well. On March 25, he wrote,

> Everything goes on prosperously. The intelligence of the men is a great surprise to me. They learn all the details of guard duty and Camp service, infinitely more readily than [the Irish] I have had under my command. There is not the least doubt, that we shall leave the state, with as good a regiment, as any that has marched.[13]

On May 25, the 54th paraded through the streets of Boston, behind a detachment of policemen, two bands, and a drum corps. Cheering crowds of blacks and whites lined the streets as abolitionist Boston turned out to see the men of the 54th Massachusetts march off to war. Vendors sold souvenirs of the historic moment, with a quote from the poet Lord Byron: "Who would be free, themselves must strike the blow."[14] William Lloyd Garrison, Frederick Douglass, Wendell Phillips, and an immensely pleased Governor Andrew were on hand as Colonel Shaw led his men past the reviewing stand.

On July 18, 1863, the men of the 54th led the Union charge on Fort Wagner, South Carolina. Six hundred of them stormed the fort under blistering fire; 272 fell dead in battle, among them Colonel Robert Gould Shaw.[15] The 54th did not take Fort Wagner, but their courageous stand proved that the sons of slaves could indeed fight for freedom: "We don't know any black men here, they're all soldiers," said one white soldier who witnessed the 54th in action.[16] An article in *Atlantic Monthly* paid respect to the fallen: "Through the cannon smoke of that dark night the manhood of the colored race shines before many eyes that would not see."[17]

The Emancipation Army

Thousands of African Americans followed in the footsteps of the 54th Massachusetts. In the North, black men enlisted in spite of racist attitudes within the military, and despite the Confederate Congress's ruling of May 1, 1863, which declared that black prisoners of war would be treated as rebelling slaves. That usually meant a death sentence.

Frederick Douglass called this "double jeopardy": death on the battlefield or death on the gallows.[18] Others followed his lead. As Douglass biographer William S. McFeely pointed out, "Jefferson Davis and his congress could have done nothing more [helpful for] gaining sympathy for black Americans from those who had never before cared about them."[19] The outcry did not go unnoticed in Washington. On July 30, 1863, President Lincoln signed an executive order instructing that "for every soldier of the United States killed in violation of the laws of war a rebel soldier shall be executed."[20]

Slaves in the strongholds of the South also worked to hasten the day of freedom. Some ran away from their masters and enlisted at the first Union encampment they could find. Others joined as contrabands, getting into the fight as Union troops pressed ever deeper into Southern territory. Those who remained in slavery had their own ways of resisting.

They bent the rules and broke the rules, slowed the pace of work, and pushed as far as they could without bringing down reprisals. African-American scholar W. E. B. DuBois called it a "general strike."[21]

When Union troops approached, slaves became more open in their defiance, refusing to obey orders or to behave in a "properly" subservient manner toward their masters. Many simply walked away from the fields, the shops, and the manor houses, to join the final push that would destroy slavery in the South.

In the spring of 1865, Union troops forced General Robert E. Lee's Southern army to abandon the Confederate lines that protected the capital of Richmond, Virginia. When the Union took the city on April 3, an African-American cavalry unit led the way. The black population of the city was on hand to cheer them. "There is no describing the scene along the route," wrote African-American reporter Thomas Morris Chester. "The colored population was wild with enthusiasm. Old men thanked God in a very boisterous manner, and old women shouted upon the pavement as high as they had done at a religious revival."[22]

Lee fled westward, but Union troops cut off his retreat. There was nowhere left to run. On April 9, 1865, Lee surrendered to General Ulysses S. Grant at the town of Appomattox Court House. Colonel Elisha Hunt Rhodes noted the momentous event in his journal:

> *Sunday April 9/64, Near Appomattox Court House, Va.—* About 11 A.M. we halted in a field . . . and stacked arms. Rumors of intended surrender were heard, but we did not

feel sure. . . . Some time in the afternoon we heard loud cheering at the front, and soon Major General Meade . . . rode like mad down the road with hat off shouting: "The war is over, and we are going home!" Such a scene only happens once in centuries. The Batteries began to fire blank cartridges, while the Infantry fired their muskets in the air. The men threw their knapsacks and canteens into the air and howled like mad. . . . I cried and laughed by turns. I never was so happy in my life.[23]

African Americans had compiled a distinguished record in the war. Nearly 180,000 served in the military, mostly in all-black units; 37,000 died in service to their country.[24]

On December 18, 1865, the dream of generations came true: The Thirteenth Amendment to the Constitution declared that neither slavery nor involuntary servitude could legally exist in the United States. Many years after the war, an elderly man gave an eloquent testimony to the slaves and sons of slaves who had helped make freedom possible: "Yes, sah! I sho does come from dat old stock who had de misfortune to be slaves, but who decided to be men, at one and de same time, and I's right proud of it."[25]

Chapter 9

THE LEGACY OF SLAVERY

Slavery was part of American life for nearly two hundred fifty years; from the first recorded sale of "twenty Negroes" in 1619 to the abolition of slavery in 1865.[1] It shaped the culture of a whole region, affected millions of lives, and very nearly destroyed the nation. Something etched so deeply into the consciousness of a people does not disappear overnight. The end of slavery did not put an end to bigotry and race hatred. Since emancipation, African Americans have faced one challenge after another in their long struggle for equality.

Rebuilding a Society

On April 14, 1865, just days after the Confederate surrender, President Abraham Lincoln was shot by John Wilkes Booth, a fanatical Southerner, at Ford's Theatre in Washington, D.C. He died the next day. Had he lived, Reconstruction—the period between the end of the war in 1865 and the withdrawal of the last Union troops from the South in 1877—might have proceeded very differently.

Lincoln had a plan for bringing the Southern states back into the Union and helping both blacks and whites adjust to a way of life that did not include slavery. Even the force of Lincoln's personality could not make this plan acceptable to everyone. Many opposed it; many more questioned it. Under Lincoln's successor, Andrew Johnson, Reconstruction became more than ever a political issue. The process that was supposed to heal the scars of disunion and slavery crippled Johnson's administration and made him the first president ever to be impeached by the House of Representatives. He came within one vote of being convicted by the Senate and removed from office.

Though Reconstructionist governments had more than their fair share of corruption and incompetence, African Americans did make some promising legal and political gains. The Civil Rights Act of 1866, passed over President Johnson's veto, extended the rights and privileges of citizenship to African Americans. In 1868, the Fourteenth Amendment incorporated this definition of citizenship into the Constitution, guaranteeing all citizens equal protection under the law. This finally corrected the gross injustice of Chief Justice Roger Taney's opinion in the *Dred Scott* case. The Fifteenth Amendment, ratified in 1870, was written to leave no doubt that the rights and privileges of citizenship included voting rights. It stated simply that the right to vote should "not be denied or abridged by the United States or by any State on account of race, color, or previous condition of servitude."[2]

During Reconstruction, sixteen African Americans were elected to Congress from Southern jurisdictions. Others served in state legislatures and in local government. These seemingly impressive advances did not outlast the

Reconstruction period. When the last Union troops pulled out of the last Southern city in 1877, the white South reasserted itself.

"Jim Crow" and the Night Riders

Nobody quite knows how the name "Jim Crow" got attached to racial segregation laws. The best guess is that it came from a character in a minstrel skit. Played by a white man in blackface makeup, Jim Crow was a bumbling, childlike caricature of African Americans.

Wherever the name came from, its meaning is clear: The post-Reconstruction South chopped itself into two unequal parts to ensure white dominance and black subservience. The strict separation of the races did not happen all at once: "White teachers were forbidden to teach black students. . . . Florida required 'Negro' textbooks and 'white' textbooks . . . Atlanta provided Jim Crow bibles for black and white witnesses."[3]

The Jim Crow system was supposed to be based on the principle of "separate but equal" facilities for the two races. In 1896, the Supreme Court ruling in the case of *Plessy* v. *Ferguson* affirmed the constitutionality of these laws. Racial segregation thus received the endorsement of the highest court in the land.

Even that was not enough to satisfy the most extreme racists. For them, separate but equal was not enough. They wanted dominance, based on nothing more than the color of their skin. Vigilantes such as the white-robed Ku Klux Klan would use any means to keep African Americans under white control.

Those who succeeded in business or other professions were in special danger of receiving a visit from the Night

Riders (a nickname for the Klan, because they generally did their raiding under cover of darkness). For example, Memphis grocer Thomas Moss made the mistake of underselling his white competition. In March 1892, an armed gang of whites burst into Moss's store. Moss and several of his friends fought back. They were arrested for their trouble.

By the time the story got to the newspapers, it had changed to portray the African Americans as the aggressors, firing on innocent whites without provocation. Vigilantes destroyed Moss's store as a warning to other blacks who might try to compete with white businesses. The grocer himself was dragged from jail and hanged, along with several of the men who had helped him protect his property.

Journalist Ida B. Wells was outraged by this savagery. Lynching—"the illegal execution of a person without any proper legal process"—was becoming all too common in the Jim Crow South.[4] Between 1882 and 1892, 728 African Americans were lynched. The problem got worse in the 1890s, with 1,217 people killed by lynch mobs.[5]

People were killed for such "crimes" as "testifying against whites in court, seeking another job, using offensive language, failing to say 'mister' to whites, disputing the price of blackberries, attempting to vote and accepting the job of postmaster."[6] White vigilantes were almost never arrested for their actions, let alone punished. When lynching cases did get to court, juries would usually find that the crime had been committed by "persons unknown to the jury."[7]

Wells organized an antilynching movement to publicize the crimes and ensure the punishment of those involved. In 1910, the antilynching crusade became a project of the newly formed National Association for the Advancement of Colored People (NAACP). Wells continued the struggle as a member of that organization's executive committee. Even with these efforts, by 1927, only thirteen states had antilynching laws on their books.

The Civil Rights Era

So long as *Plessy* v. *Ferguson* legalized separate-but-equal segregation, African Americans had nowhere to turn. For legal remedies even to begin, the *Plessy* ruling would first have to be rejected. That did not happen until 1954, when NAACP attorney (and future Supreme Court justice) Thurgood Marshall argued the case of *Brown* v. *Board of Education of Topeka, Kansas,* before the United States Supreme Court. The case concerned an African-American child who was suing for the right to attend a white school in segregated Topeka, Kansas. *Brown* challenged the separate-but-equal doctrine.

On Monday, May 17, 1954, at 12:52 P.M., Chief Justice Earl Warren read the opinion of the Court. Warren biographer Ed Cray described the scene:

> There was no hint in the first pages of the opinion just how the Court would rule. Warren read on, steadily, the tension in the marble courtroom growing.
>
> "We come then to the question presented," Warren read. "Does segregation of children in public schools solely on the basis of race . . . deprive the children of the minority group of equal educational opportunities?"
>
> He barely paused. "We unanimously believe that it does."[8]

A new era began. The concept of separate-but-equal had been cast aside, and with it the foundation of Jim Crow segregation. The civil rights movement had begun.

Throughout the 1950s and 1960s, African Americans and their supporters challenged racial bias on every level. Many people stepped forward to lead the way: Rosa Parks, who triggered the famous Montgomery, Alabama, bus boycott of 1956 when she refused to give up her seat to a white man; Reverend Martin Luther King, Jr., whose firm leadership and commitment to nonviolence inspired a vast national movement; Malcolm X, the militant who turned peace-maker; Jesse Jackson, the flamboyant young minister who brought a message of hope in a violent time.

Jim Crow laws slowly began to disappear as African Americans established their rights under the law. Many believed that the legacy of slavery was at last ended. Others did not agree. A real end to racism would require more than a change in law: It would require a change in "the hearts and minds of men," as one of Earl Warren's law clerks once reminded the Chief Justice.[9]

Racism has continued to flare up, sometimes in the most unexpected situations. Every time the spiritual heirs of the old abolitionists start believing that the battle has at last been won, something occurs to smash that belief. In 1988, David Duke, a former Grand Dragon of the Ku Klux Klan, ran openly for president as the candidate of the Populist party. He received over 47,000 votes.[10] In 1991, African-American motorist Rodney King was stopped for speeding and savagely beaten by members of the Los Angeles police department. In 1998, residents of Jasper, Texas, were stunned by a particularly vicious murder: James Byrd, Jr., was dragged behind a truck and killed, his body literally torn apart. A young man convicted of the murder in February 1999 was a member of a racist organization called the Aryan Brotherhood.

Such horrors remind us that the real legacy of slavery is not racial discrimination or segregation but racial hatred. On that, Chief Justice Earl Warren's law clerk was right: We have a long way to go.

☆ TIMELINE ☆

1619—First recorded sale of slaves in American colonies.

1784—Pennsylvania Society for the Abolition of Slavery founded.

1800—*August*: Gabriel Prosser plans slave revolt.

1804—*January 1*: Jean-Jacques Dessalines proclaims free Republic of Haiti.

1807—*May 1*: Great Britain bans international slave trade.

1808—*January 1*: United States bans international slave trade.

1822—*July*: Denmark Vesey plans slave revolt.

1831—*January 1*: William Lloyd Garrison publishes first issue of *The Liberator*.

August 31: Nat Turner leads slave revolt in Virginia.

1833—*December*: American Anti-Slavery Society founded.

1839—*April*: Revolt aboard the slave ship *Amistad*.

1841—*March 9*: Supreme Court frees the *Amistad* rebels.

1850—Fugitive Slave Law passed.

1852—*Uncle Tom's Cabin* published.

1854—*May 30*: Congress passes Kansas-Nebraska Act.

1859—*October 16*: John Brown's raid on Harpers Ferry, Virginia.

1861—*March 4*: Abraham Lincoln inaugurated president.

April 12: Firing on Fort Sumter begins Civil War.

1863—*January 1*: Emancipation Proclamation issued.

July 18: Assault on Fort Wagner by 54th Massachusetts.

1865—*March 4*: Lincoln's second inauguration.

April 9: Lee surrenders at Appomattox.

April 14: Lincoln assassinated.

December: Thirteenth Amendment ends slavery.

1868—*July*: Fourteenth Amendment gives citizenship to former slaves.

1870—*March*: Fifteenth Amendment confirms voting rights of African Americans.

1896—*Plessy* v. *Ferguson* affirms Jim Crow laws.

1954—*May 17*: In *Brown* v. *Board of Education*, Supreme Court finds that racial segregation denies equal opportunity; Civil rights movement begins.

☆ CHAPTER NOTES ☆

Chapter 1. A Thousand Miles for Freedom

1. William and Ellen Craft, *Running a Thousand Miles for Freedom*, Project Gutenberg, Etext #585, <http://www.gutenberg.net/>, n.p.

2. Ibid.

Chapter 2. The Peculiar Institution

1. Peter Kolchin, *American Slavery, 1619–1877* (New York: Hill and Wang, 1993), p. 93.

2. Hugh Thomas, *The Slave Trade: The Story of the Atlantic Slave Trade, 1440–1870* (New York: Simon & Schuster, 1997), p. 51.

3. Ibid., p. 59.

4. Bruce Levine, *Half Slave and Half Free: The Roots of Civil War* (New York: Hill and Wang, 1992), p. 19.

5. Thomas, p. 174.

6. *U.S. Declaration of Independence*, prepared for cybercasting by Gerald Murphy (The Cleveland Free-Net). National Public Telecomputing Network. n.p., n.d.

7. Howard Jones, *Mutiny on the* Amistad: *The Saga of a Slave Revolt and Its Impact on American Abolition, Law, and Diplomacy* (New York: Oxford University Press, 1987), p. 14.

8. Thomas, p. 411.

9. Robert Walsh, "A Slave Ship in the South Atlantic," May 24, 1829, in David Colbert, ed., *Eyewitness to America: 500 Years of America in the Words of Those Who Saw It Happen* (New York: Pantheon Books, 1997), p. 136.

10. Kolchin, p. 4.

11. Ibid., p. 7.

12. Ibid., p. 15.

13. J. H. Plumb, quoted in Allen Weinstein and Frank Otto Gatell, eds., *American Negro Slavery: A Modern Reader* (New York: Oxford University Press, 1968), p. 405.

14. Kolchin, p. 242.

Chapter 3. People as Property

1. Bruce Levine, *Half Slave and Half Free: The Roots of Civil War* (New York: Hill and Wang, 1992), p. 22.

2. Ibid.

3. Ibid., p. 148.

4. Ibid.

5. Peter Kolchin, *American Slavery, 1619–1877* (New York: Hill and Wang, 1993), p. 112.

6. Letter from John Ball to John Ball, Jr., October 6, 1801, quoted in Edward Ball, *Slaves in the Family* (New York: Farrar, Strauss and Giroux, 1998), pp. 245–246.

7. Douglas R. Egerton, *Gabriel's Rebellion: The Virginia Slave Conspiracies of 1800 & 1802* (Chapel Hill: The University of North Carolina Press, 1993), p. 219 (n. 50).

8. Ibid., p. 111.

9. Martin Ros, *Night of Fire: The Black Napoleon and the Battle of Haiti*, ed. Karin Ford-Treep (New York: Sarpedon, 1994), p. 197.

Chapter 4. Matters of Conscience

1. Quoted in John Chester Miller, *The Wolf by the Ears: Thomas Jefferson and Slavery* (New York: New American Library, 1977), p. 8.

2. Bruce Levine, *Half Slave and Half Free: The Roots of Civil War* (New York: Hill and Wang, 1992), p. 82.

3. Charles G. Finney, "Self Deceivers," *Lectures to Professing Christians*, 1878, <http://ccel.wheaton.edu/finney/lectures/> n.p., (July 16, 1998).

4. Eric Foner and John A. Garraty, eds., *The Reader's Companion to American History* (New York: Houghton Mifflin Co., 1991), Electronic version, 1998, Infonautics Corporation, n.p.

5. Philip S. Foner, *History of Black Americans: From the Emergence of the Cotton Kingdom to the Eve of the Compromise of 1850* (Westport, Conn.: Greenwood Press, 1983), vol. 2, p. 390.

6. Henry Mayer, *All on Fire: William Lloyd Garrison and the Abolition of Slavery* (New York: St. Martin's Press, 1998), p. xiii.

7. *The Confessions of Nat Turner*, in *A Hypertext in American History: From the Colonial Period to Modern Times*, <http://odur.let.rug.nl/~usa/>, n.p., (August 10, 1998).

8. Ibid.

9. Benjamin Quarles, *Turner, Nat (1800–1831)*, vol. 22, *Colliers Encyclopedia* CD-ROM, February 28, 1996. Copyright Infonautics Corporation, 1998, n.p.

10. Ibid., p. 40.

11. Quoted in Alan L. Stoskopf and Margaret Stern Strom, *Choosing to Participate: A Critical Examination of Citizenship in American History* (Brookline, Mass.: Facing History and Ourselves, 1990), p. 147.

12. Ibid.

13. Martin Zapata, "News and Views: The Father of Scientific Racism," *The Journal of Blacks in Higher Education*, June 30, 1995, pp. PG.

14. Foner, *History of Black Americans*, vol. 2, p. 370.

15. Ibid.

Chapter 5. Fighting the Good Fight

1. Frederick Douglass, *My Bondage and Freedom*, Electronic version (Champagne, Ill.: Project Gutenberg, January 1995), n.p.

2. James Mellon, ed., *Bullwhip Days, The Slaves Remember: An Oral History* (New York: Avon Books, 1988), p. 247.

3. Ibid., p. 244.

4. Ibid., p. 239.

5. Quoted in George P. Rawick, ed., *The American Slave: A Composite Autobiography* (Westport, Conn.: Greenwood Publishing Co., 1972), vol. 5, pp. 62–65.

6. Quoted in Mellon, p. 287.

7. Peter Kolchin, *American Slavery, 1619–1877* (New York: Hill and Wang, 1993), p. 97.

8. Kenneth M. Stampp, *The Peculiar Institution* (New York: Vintage Books, 1956), p. 82.

9. Quoted in Stampp, p. 85.

10. Dorothy Sterling, *Ahead of Her Time: Abby Kelley and the Politics of Antislavery* (New York: W. W. Norton & Co., 1991), p. 105.

11. Ibid., pp. 13–14.

12. Quoted in Sterling, p. 153.

13. William Lloyd Garrison, Preface to Frederick Douglass, *Narrative of the Life of Frederick Douglass, an American Slave, Written by Himself* (Boston: Anti-Slavery Office, 1845), n.p.

14. Ibid.

15. William S. McFeely, *Frederick Douglass* (New York: W. W. Norton, 1991), p. 143.

16. Quoted in Nall Irvin Painter, *Sojourner Truth: A Life, A Symbol* (New York: W. W. Norton & Co., 1996), p. 105.

17. Ibid., p. 114.

Chapter 6. Traveling the Freedom Road

1. Quoted in Howard Jones, *Mutiny on the* Amistad: *The Saga of a Slave Revolt and Its Impact on American Abolition, Law, and Diplomacy* (New York: Oxford University Press, 1987), p. 42.

2. Jones, p. 219.

3. Ibid., p. 220.

4. Philip S. Foner, *History of Black Americans: From the Emergence of the Cotton Kingdom to the Eve of the Compromise of 1850* (Westport, Conn.: Greenwood Press, 1983), vol. 2, p. 482.

5. Stuart Seely Sprague, ed., *His Promised Land: The Autobiography of John P. Parker, Former Slave and Conductor on the Underground Railroad* (New York: W. W. Norton, 1996), p. 86.

6. Ibid., p. 9.

7. Steven Mintz, ed., *Excerpts from Slave Narratives* (Houston, Tex.: University of Houston), n.d., <http://vi.uh.edu/pages/mintz/primary.htm>, #35.

8. *Compton's New Century Encyclopedia*, CD-ROM (Compton's NewMedia, Inc., 1994), n.p.

9. Sprague, p. 138.

10. Quoted in *Compton's Interactive Encyclopedia* (Compton's NewMedia, Inc., 1993), n.p.

11. Quoted in Levine, p. 174.

12. Ibid., p. 175.

13. Henry David Thoreau, "Civil Disobedience," in *Civil Disobedience and Other Essays* (New York: Dover Publications, Inc., 1993), p. 9.

14. Quoted in Levine, pp. 177–178.

15. Levine, p. 178.

Chapter 7. The Conflict Deepens

1. Dorothy Sterling, *Ahead of Her Time: Abby Kelley and the Politics of Antislavery* (New York: W. W. Norton & Co., 1991), p. 293n.

2. Bruce Levine, *Half Slave and Half Free: The Roots of Civil War* (New York: Hill and Wang, 1992), p. 190.

3. Andrew Delbanco, "Harriet Beecher Stowe: A Life," *The New Republic*, April 18, 1994, vol. 210, p. 38 (7).

4. Ibid.

5. "John Brown's Raid: Chapter 1, The Road to Harpers Ferry," *U.S. History*, September 1, 1990 (Electric Library, Infonautics Corporation, 1998), n.p.

6. Eric Foner and John A. Garraty, eds., *The Reader's Companion to American History* (New York: Houghton Mifflin Co., 1991), Electronic version, 1998, Infonautics Corporation, n.p.

7. "John Brown's Raid," n.p.

8. Ibid.

9. Linn Washington, "Scott case is a shameful chapter in U.S. Supreme Court history," *The Philadelphia Tribune*, February 7, 1995, Electronic version, Ethnic NewsWatch. Softline Information, Inc., Stamford, Conn.

10. Chief Justice Robert B. Taney, Opinion re: *Dred Scott, Plaintiff in error,* v. *John F. A. Sanford.* Supreme Court of the United States (Howard vol. 19, p. 393, December 1856 term). Electronic version, <http://www.alaska.net/~winter/dred_scott.html>, (June 20, 1998).

11. Ibid.

12. Ibid.

13. "John Brown's Raid," n.p.

Chapter 8. War and Abolition

1. Quoted in *The Columbia Encyclopedia*, 5th ed. (New York: Columbia University Press, 1993), Electronic version, copyright 1987, Infonautics Corporation, n.p.

2. "Lincoln's First Inaugural Address. March 4, 1861," prepared by Gerald Murphy (The Cleveland Free-Net). National Public Telecomputing Network, n.p., n.d.

3. Quoted in Bruce Levine, *Half Slave and Half Free: The Roots of Civil War* (New York: Hill and Wang, 1992), p. 224.

4. Ibid.

5. Ibid.

6. Ibid., p. 239.

7. William S. McFeely, *Frederick Douglass* (New York: W. W. Norton, 1991), p. 212.

8. "The Emancipation Proclamation," prepared by Gerald Murphy (The Cleveland Free-Net). National Public Telecomputing Network, n.p., n.d.

9. Quoted in McFeely, pp. 215–216.

10. Douglas T. Miller, Notes to "The Emancipation Proclamation," prepared by Gerald Murphy (The Cleveland Free-Net). National Public Telecomputing Network, n.p., n.d., (August 28, 1998).

11. "The Emancipation Proclamation," prepared by Gerald Murphy (The Cleveland Free-Net). National Public Telecomputing Network, n.p., n.d., (August 28, 1998).

12. Russell Duncan, ed., *Blue-Eyed Child of Fortune: The Civil War Letters of Colonel Robert Gould Shaw* (Athens, Ga. and London: The University of Georgia Press, 1992), p. 21.

13. Ibid., p. 313.

14. Quoted in George Seldes, *The Great Thoughts* (New York: Ballantine Books, 1985), p. 62.

15. Duncan, p. 52.

16. Quoted in Anna Mary Wells, *Dear Preceptor: The Life and Times of Thomas Wentworth Higginson* (Boston: Houghton Mifflin, 1963), p. 180.

17. Quoted in Lawrence Lader, *The Bold Brahmins: New England's War Against Slavery, 1831–1863* (New York: E. P. Dutton, 1961), p. 290.

18. McFeely, p. 228.

19. Ibid.

20. Ibid.

21. Peter Kolchin, *American Slavery, 1619–1877* (New York: Hill and Wang, 1993), p. 203.

22. Quoted in Nick Salvatore, *We All Got History: The Memory Books of Amos Webber* (New York: Times Books, 1996), p. 144.

23. Robert Hunt Rhodes, ed., *All for the Union: The Civil War Diary and Letters of Elisha Hunt Rhodes* (New York: Orion Books, 1985), pp. 229–230.

24. Duncan, p. 20.

25. Quoted in James Mellon, ed., *Bullwhip Days, The Slaves Remember: An Oral History* (New York: Avon Books, 1988), p. 460.

Chapter 9. The Legacy of Slavery

1. Hugh Thomas, *The Slave Trade: The Story of the Atlantic Slave Trade, 1440–1870* (New York: Simon & Schuster, 1997), p. 174.

2. Quoted in Peter Kolchin, *American Slavery, 1619–1877* (New York: Hill and Wang, 1993), p. 211.

3. Lerone Bennett, Jr., *Before the Mayflower: A History of Black America* (Chicago: Johnson Publishing Company, 1982), pp. 256–257.

4. Alan L. Stoskopf and Margaret Stern Strom, *Choosing to Participate: A Critical Examination of*

Citizenship in American History (Brookline, Mass.: Facing History and Ourselves, 1990), p. 113.

5. Ibid., p. 114.

6. Bennett, p. 271.

7. Leon F. Litwack, *Trouble in Mind: Black Southerners in the Age of Jim Crow* (New York: Alfred A. Knopf, 1998), p. 295.

8. Ed Cray, *Chief Justice: A Biography of Earl Warren* (New York: Simon & Schuster, 1997), p. 287.

9. Ibid., p. 524.

10. *Compton's New Century Encyclopedia* (Compton's NewMedia, 1994), n.p.

☆ FURTHER READING ☆

Books

Hamilton, Virginia. *Many Thousand Gone: African Americans from Slavery to Freedom*. New York: Knopf Books for Young Readers, 1993.

Jacobs, Harriet A. *Incidents in the Life of a Slave Girl: Written By Herself*. Cambridge, Mass.: Harvard University Press, 1987.

Lester, Julius. *Long Journey Home: Stories From Black History*. New York: Dial Books for Young Readers, 1993.

McNeese, Tim. *The Abolitionist Movement: Ending Slavery*. New York: Chelsea House Publishers, 2007.

Parker, John. *His Promised Land: The Autobiography of John P. Parker, Former Slave and Conductor on the Underground Railroad*. New York: W. W. Norton & Co., 1996.

Paulson, Timothy J. *Days of Sorrow, Years of Glory 1813–1850: From the Nat Turner Revolt to the Fugitive Slave Law*. New York: Chelsea House, 1994.

Riehecky, Janet. *The Emancipation Proclamation: The Abolition of Slavery*. Portsmouth, N.H.: Heinemann Library, 2002.

☆ INDEX ☆